CENTER

PLSTA

1006600614

The Right Choice

The Right

edited by Paul T. Stallsworth

Choice

PRO-LIFE SERMONS FROM

Elizabeth Achtemeier
Connie Roland Alt
John B. Brown
Paul M. Clark
Edward Fehskens
Michael J. Gorman
Richard John Neuhaus
John Cardinal O'Connor
Frank A. Pavone
Terry Schlossberg
Benjamin E. Sheldon
Paul T. Stallsworth
Mother Teresa of Calcutta
and Charles E. Whited, Jr.

ABINGDON PRESS
NASHVILLE

THE RIGHT CHOICE

Copyright © 1997 by Abingdon Press

This book is printed on recycled, acid-free, elemental chlorine–free paper.

Scripture quotations, unless otherwise noted, are from the Revised Standard Version of the Bible, copyright 1946, 1952, 1971 by the Division of Christian Education of the National Council of the Churches of Christ in the United States of America. Used by permission.

Scripture quotations noted NRSV are from the New Revised Standard Version Bible, copyright © 1989, by the Division of Christian Education of the National Council of the Churches of Christ in the United States of America.

ISBN 0-687-05079-0

Library of Congress Cataloging-in-Publication Data

The right choice / edited by Paul T. Stallsworth : pro-life sermons
    from Elizabeth Achtemeier . . . [et al.].
        p.   cm.
    Includes bibliographical references.
    ISBN 0-687-05079-0 (pbk. : alk. paper)
    1. Abortion—Religious aspects—Christianity—Sermons. 2. Pro-life movement—
Moral and ethical aspects.   I. Stallsworth, Paul T.   II. Achtemeier, Elizabeth Rice,
1926–
    HQ767.25.R54 1997
    241'.6976—dc21   96-51889
                                                                                                              CIP

97 98 99 00 01 02 03 04 05 06—10 9 8 7 6 5 4 3 2 1

MANUFACTURED IN THE UNITED STATES OF AMERICA

To Marsha,
sister in Christ,
beloved wife,
and good mother

Contents

Foreword

Abortion—along with euthanasia, genetic engineering, and eugenics—is a societal tragedy that seems not to let up. As such, abortion is a problem that confronts all the churches in the United States. For this reason, the National Pro-life Religious Council (NPRC) was formed. The NPRC's mission was, is, and will be to provide ecumenical witness, in word and deed, that reflects the historic Christian understanding of the dignity of human life.

This collection of sermons—ably edited by the Reverend Paul T. Stallsworth, a member of the NPRC's board of directors—is an effort to express that Christian understanding with regard to abortion. It is a step toward finding our collective, our ecumenical, voice. It makes clear that the Christian churches here represented are seeking to inform and form their people in the context of worship, according to the revelation offered to the world through the Word of God.

We realize that some pastors have chosen, for various reasons, to remain silent concerning the forces that contribute to what Pope John Paul II has termed the "culture of death." Silence, however, is not for us. Where God has spoken, we must speak, as best we can. In doing so, we hope that this slim volume will be a means of encouraging others—clergy and laity—to break silence and to sound forth the Word of God regarding life and abortion. This Word is the truth that provides the basis for our freedom as human beings: male and female, young and old, black and white, disabled and able-bodied, born and unborn.

We also hope that this effort will contribute in some measure to Christian unity and cooperation. We cannot deny that there are differences among and within the churches. But that there is vast common ground in faith and practice is cause for great joy. It is on this basis that we choose to speak, to act, and to contribute to an emerging culture of life.

The Reverend John B. Brown
President, National Pro-life Religious Council

Introduction

The idea for this book first arose about four years ago. As three United Methodist pastors (including this one) were engaged in theological conversation over lunch in a Raleigh restaurant, one proposed that a book of pro-life sermons would be quite helpful to the working pastor, as well as lay leaders and Sunday school teachers, in the local church.

A couple of years later, the same proposal—a book of pro-life sermons—received the institutional boost and encouragement it required. The proposal was outlined and discussed among pro-life leaders at a meeting of the National Pro-life Religious Council (NPRC) in Sterling, Virginia, just west of Washington, D.C.

The NPRC is an ecumenical organization that acknowledges Jesus Christ as Lord and Savior, and is called to affirm and witness to the biblical standard of the dignity and sanctity of human life. The council consists of pro-life leaders from various Christian communions across the nation. These leaders represent their Orthodox, Protestant, and Roman Catholic pro-life organizations; and they come together to exchange ideas and information.

The NPRC's board of directors, meeting in Sterling, adopted this book proposal as a long-term project. At the same meeting, the board also selected one of its own, this pastor, to compile and edit this collection of sermons.

Within weeks after the formal adoption of this book proposal, sermon manuscripts were requested from most of the leaders of the NPRC, as well as selected others. In response, manuscripts came in from across the communions and the country. The "sermons" (quotation marks are employed here because Dr. Achtemeier's "sermon" is actually an essay on the writing of sermons on life and abortion, and Rev. Neuhaus's "sermon" is more like a speech on public philosophy with theological content) selected for publication in this volume are from laity, pastors, priests, and professors. They are from men and women from the Evangelical Lutheran Church in America, the Lutheran Church—Missouri Synod, the Presbyterian Church (U.S.A.), the Roman Catholic Church, The United Methodist Church, and the United Church of Christ. Due to the number of communions that are represented, this volume is most definitely ecumenical in orientation. Moreover, this volume is ecumenical in the sense that it attempts to set forth the historic ecumenical consensus on life and abortion that the Church, at her most faithful, has transmitted through the ages. This ecumenical consensus includes both catholic substance and evangelical aspiration.

The ecumenical nature of this collection of sermons is most important, for it displays decisively, if not conclusively, that faithfulness to the Christian gospel includes faithful protection of innocent human life. To be more specific, to be faithfully Christian is to be faithfully protective of the unborn child and mother. Most simply stated, to be Christian is to be pro-life. (This does not mean, of course, that pro-choice or pro-abortion church people should, of necessity, be removed from the Christian community. But it does mean that those who preach, teach, and follow the historic ecumenical consensus on abortion should seek to persuade, to speak "the truth in love" [Eph. 4:15], to these brothers and sisters.)

In these last days of the twentieth century, it is becoming increasingly apparent to many that the Christian faith is more about communal truth than individual experience, more about faithfulness than choice, more about discipleship than self-expression. In these days just prior to the arrival of the third millennium, churches that have tried to be pro-choice in various aspects of their lives—from content of worship, to biblical interpretation, to doctrine, to abortion, and now to physician-assisted suicide—are finding that choice cannot bind and hold together people in the gospel. Only the Truth named Jesus Christ, through Word and Sacraments, can do that; and that Truth and his binding have more than a little to do with life and abortion.

If you are unconvinced that the gospel is linked with the protection of life, read the sermons that follow to be challenged, and perhaps persuaded, to reconsider your position. If you are already persuaded that the gospel is linked with the protection of life, read the following sermons to be strengthened in the position and mission of historic Christianity.

An Unfortunate Title

An admission is in order. The editor of this book is not particularly fond of the title that Abingdon Press has assigned. At its beginning, this book proposal carried the title *Sermons for the Church: On Life and Abortion.* But for marketing reasons and others, Abingdon changed the title to *The Right Choice: Pro-Life Sermons from . . .*

"Why," one might inquire, "does *The Right Choice* give offense?"

Three points should be offered in reply. First, the word *right*—at least in the highly politicized setting of American society in the mid-1990s—suggests the political right more than moral or theological rightness. And that is a problem. For this book is not, by intention, partisan-political. Nor is this book, in fact, partisan-political. The intent of this book is to transcend, and call to judgment, the political right and the political left, conservatives and liberals, Republicans and Democrats, and other political parties and philosophies that are alive and well in contemporary American political culture. Even so, though this book does not intend to further a partisan-political agenda, it does have strong implications for how the general society ought to order its life together (which is what politics, at its best, is all about).

Second, the word *right* might give some the idea that the contributors to this little book consider themselves absolutely correct on the matter of life and abortion. Some might even suggest that we think we possess the truth regarding life and abortion. This perception would be inaccurate. This volume's contributors believe themselves to be in service of the Truth; but that, needless to say, does not make us perfect possessors of absolute truth. We know that we are sinners in thought and word and deed, in need of forgiveness—even when it comes to our witness on life and abortion. We know that we are hypocrites— saints and sinners at once, according to Martin Luther—whose words are much better than our deeds.

However strange it may seem, we believe that hypocrisy, which involves falling short of given standards, is better than the nihilism that is gradually gaining ground in U.S. churches and in the general society. Today's nihilism, to the detriment of all, involves no given standards whatsoever. Hence, in our setting, it is becoming increasingly daring to be a hypocrite over against the nihilism of the hour.

And third, *choice* is one of the most overused words in the United States. It is used to sell everything under the sun—from self-help methods to U.S. Senate candidates to soft drinks. That is probably one reason those who call themselves "pro-choice," who favor abortion on demand in American society, have laid claim to the word. It seems to this editor that, in North American culture, whenever the word *choice* is employed, the pro-choice philosophy is thereby given advantage and reinforcement, even if subtly. Therefore, a title without the word *choice* would have been preferable.

So what are we to make of the title *The Right Choice*? We should, and will, make the best of it. The contributors to this book believe that for a woman in a difficult pregnancy there really is a right choice, based on the Christian promise, the Christian reality. In other words, we believe that, according to the Christian faith, the choices confronting this woman are not morally equal; we believe that, on the basis of the Christian gospel, the choice to nurture the life of the unborn child and to protect the mother from abortion is morally superior to all other choices. This choice involves much more than one good decision made by one autonomous woman; for it involves faith in the God of the Bible, hope in the God who provides in all circumstances, love for the God who creates all the children of the world, willingness to recognize tradition and truth, and the participation of a church or of Christian disciples willing to welcome a distressed woman with child. This choice, the right choice, which is the faithful choice, brings honor to the God who creates, redeems, and sustains human beings. This choice is a sign of the Kingdom of God, the Kingdom that is coming in glory and power.

Acknowledgments

For their participation in this project, I would like to publicly thank the thirteen other contributors to this volume. In addition, I am eager to acknowledge the good and energetic labors of my colleague Linda Beecher, the secretary at the Rose Hill United Methodist Church. I wish to express gratitude to the church I serve, the Rose Hill United Methodist Church, for providing a genuine Christian community that makes a project such as this possible. That Christian community is also found among the pastors of the Rose Hill community and the United Methodist pastors of the Goldsboro District, led by District Superintendent James C. Lee. I am truly indebted to Ruth Brown of Dothan, Alabama, and Steve Wissler of Ephrata, Pennsylvania, for steady friendship and continuing collaboration over the years.

This book required many late nights in the pastor's study, especially during the summer of 1995. Marsha, my faithful wife, and our children—Ryan, Paige, Matthew, and Peter—were understanding and supportive beyond the call of duty, the vast majority of the time.

One last word of thanks is due, and that is to the current Bishop of Rome. John Paul II's clear, consistent, and courageous witness—eloquently demonstrated in his eleventh encyclical, *Evangelium Vitae* (*The Gospel of Life*)—has given abundant inspiration to clergy and laity across the churches, including this pastor. Truly, this Pope speaks the Word of God to the universal Church and to the world.

The contributors to this book hope that its content will give strong assistance and comfort to clergy, laity, and congregations that are offering "the Gospel of Life" to a world increasingly tempted and seduced by a "culture of death."

Paul T. Stallsworth
Fourth Sunday of Easter 1996
Rose Hill, North Carolina

The Right Choice

Chapter 1
Speaking the Unspeakable:
A Demonstration

Elizabeth Achtemeier

We preachers often find ourselves up against the necessity of preaching about one of the difficult, pressing issues of the day. Take the issue of abortion, for example. From the pulpit few of us dare touch the issue, because it is much too controversial. Everyone in our congregation either has an opinion about it or does not wish to discuss it. Certainly, some women in the congregation have had abortions or know someone who has. And were we to preach about abortion from the standpoint of the Scriptures, we would do nothing but arouse angry feelings among our people and perhaps divide them into warring camps. Therefore, we conclude, it would be much better to leave the subject to the hardcore evangelicals or to the crazies who attack abortion clinics, and just get on with our efforts to build up our congregations in harmony and love.

The difficulty, of course, is that the issue is being forced upon us by the events of our time and place. If we are astute observers of the societal scene, it is clear that human life is growing cheaper and cheaper in the United States. The newspapers are full of tales of assisted suicide, euthanasia, and adequate medical care denied to the elderly. Abortion is just one more piece of evidence of our readiness to take into our own hands decisions about who shall live and who shall die.

Every year around 1.5 million unborn children end up as "medical waste" in this country, with over 36 million since the United States Supreme Court decision of *Roe v. Wade* in 1973. And of course the freedom to increase that number at will is now seen as a woman's right. Pamela Maraldo, the former president of the Planned Parenthood Federation of America, the largest abortion provider in the United States, says: "Abortion is where the rubber hits the road, the line in the sand for women to become fully equal citizens."[1] Her implication is that women become sexually equal to men through the freedom to kill their unborn children. Surely the Christian faith—with its understandings of where true freedom lies, with its standards of sexual morality, and with its concerns for the most helpless among us—has something to say from the Gospel to that attitude.

Theological Reasoning from the Text

How do we begin? It is necessary in topical preaching, as in every type of preaching, to begin with a text; and certainly the central text when dealing with abortion is the commandment from the Decalogue, "You shall not kill" (Exod. 20:13). But it is meditation on the theological *reasons* for that command that aids the preacher in filling out the content of the topical sermon.

The Doctrine of Creation

We Christian preachers always start with the presupposition that God in Jesus Christ's relationship to the world, to all people, is the most important reality in history and nature. When we are dealing with abortion, this presupposition does not change.

The triune God is the author of all life on this planet, we affirm, and thus the creator of human life in the womb. That theological fact immediately eliminates our society's endless arguments over when human life begins, for it cannot be denied that when a woman's egg is penetrated by a man's sperm in the woman's fallopian tube to form a zygote, God has set out to create a human being. To be sure, early on it does not look human to us, but it contains the forty-six chromosomes necessary to develop into a unique and unrepeatable person.

God has extended his arm to give the gift of a child, and the only question is whether we will brush aside the arm and refuse the gift, or gratefully accept it from God's grace. When we speak about abortion, we are dealing with what God the Creator has given.

The Doctrine of Redemption

We preachers are also dealing with that which belongs to God. We confess in the biblical faith, "The earth is the LORD's and all that is in it, / the world, and those who live in it" (Ps. 24:1 NRSV). We do not belong to ourselves. Abortion advocates live by the creed that says, "My body is my own," but everything in the Christian faith contradicts that faithless claim. "It is he that made us, and we are his," sings the psalmist (100:3).

Indeed, when we try to deny that and to become autonomous and self-governing, God sends his Son to find and reclaim us as his beloved children (John 1:12-13; Gal. 4:4-7). And so, says Paul, "You are not your own; you were bought with a price" (1 Cor. 6:19b-20a). The Church affirms that fact every time we baptize a child or an adult. This baptized person now belongs to God, we claim, and therefore nothing in all creation can now separate this child of the covenant from the love of God in Christ Jesus our Lord (Rom. 8:38-39). All life that God creates, whether in the womb or out of it, belongs to our one Creator and Redeemer. Therefore, since mere mortals should not exercise supreme lordship over life, they are not free to rob God of what belongs to him.

Surely that fact—that our children belong to God and not to us—lies at the basis of all Christian parenthood. So daily we lift our children up in prayer before the Father and beg his guidance and protection of them. And daily we seek to "bring them up in the discipline and instruction of the Lord" (Eph. 6:4). We nurture them, by word and example, to walk in ways pleasing to God, so that they do not fall into the deadly slavery that characterizes our sex-saturated culture (see 1 Cor. 7:23).

The Doctrine of the Church

We Christians further confess that we are our "brother's keeper" (Gen. 4:9); that we are responsible to God for loving our neighbor, whom God loves; and that we "fulfil the law of Christ" by "bear[ing] one another's burdens" (Gal. 6:2). That is the Church's answer to our heedless society's rationalizations that claim it is better for some children not to be born. The problem of the pregnant fifteen-year-old in our midst is no longer, in the love of Christ, simply *her* problem. It is *our* problem—the congregation's problem. And the problem of the poverty-stricken, the abused, and the unwanted child is the anguished call to the church in every community to get to work to save its children. We do not avoid God's condemnation of the Church by supporting, or aiding in, the abortion of such children; we magnify it. As Mother Teresa once said, "If you do not want the child, give him to me; I want him." That surely is the readiness of faith with which the Body of Christ must gird itself in this age of unrestricted abortion.

Thus, in this fashion, working out of the *sensus fidelium*—out of the apostolic faith of the Church—does the preacher fill out a sermon on a thorny topic like abortion, and bring the gospel to bear on the attitudes and practices of the day.

Practical Results of the Sermon

Every preacher hopes, when dealing with a pressing issue of the day, to produce practical results in the life of the congregation and in the lives of its members. That is, the preacher hopes to spur the hearers to action or at least to work some change in their attitudes that will eventually lead to action. Ernest Campbell used to recommend that after every sermon on a social-action issue a table be stationed in the vestibule where parishioners could sign up to go to work on the problem addressed.

Therefore, with respect to abortion, the preacher may wish to enlist names for a congregational committee to deal with problem pregnancies. Certainly the formation of such a group would signal the willingness of the congregation to receive into its fellowship and care those who have formerly been shunned—the unmarried and promiscuous teenager, the scared and pregnant college student, the welfare client, the impoverished. Such a committee, supported by the awakened congregation, would take upon itself the responsibility for enabling a woman to avoid the tragedy of abortion. Many women who have submitted to abortion have done so only because they thought there was no one to help them. But any congregation that decides it will tackle the problem of abortion can furnish that invaluable help. In short, a church can demonstrate Christian love's willingness to be burdened with someone else's problems.

For those pregnant women who need it, the problem pregnancy committee can arrange baby showers and clothes closets, medical and financial help, job training, education, counseling, housing, and aid with adoption when desired.

Most important, the congregation that decides to work to save the lives of little ones and their mothers also takes upon itself the responsibility of so living as the Body of Christ that the pregnant woman, and then her baby, might become disciples of our Lord. Jesus Christ was born to an unwed, betrothed teenager and laid in a cattle manger. When he was a man, Jesus said he had nowhere to lay his head. The church of this Jesus, this Lord, should know how to welcome into its midst all those helpless ones who know the same poverty.

Avoiding Moralism

We preachers must preach about sin. And in a society that does not believe in sin and thinks that anything goes, it is a necessity to keep before our congregations the reality and seriousness of God's commandments. We preachers, above all others, are given the task of picturing all of life in relationship to God. Because of this divine/human relationship, our Lord has made it very clear through the Scriptures that his commandments are to be obeyed, that he cannot be mocked, and that we will reap what we sow (Gal. 6:7-8).

In dealing with the text of Exodus 20:13, the preacher must first explain to the congregation the Christian reasons for the commandment, "You shall not kill." In addition, he or she must point the congregation toward some practical solutions about what to do in response. Then some of the theological and practical suggestions I have discussed above may be utilized in the sermon.

But the Christian preacher, to avoid finally sinking into moralism, must also explain to the congregation that God's commandments are not heavy, legalistic demands that are unmercifully laid upon us. Rather, they are God's gracious guidance of us in the new life that he has given us in Jesus Christ.

We do not work our way into relationship with God. Every person who claims the name *Christian* should know that. "While we were yet sinners Christ died for us" (Rom. 5:8). This redemption was accomplished by the Cross and Resurrection of Jesus Christ. The Atonement was made. God himself, in his Son, reopened our way into his presence and reconciled us to himself, thus enabling us to live in peace with him and with one another. Further, he poured into our hearts the Spirit of Christ, and thereby gave us the power to live righteous lives and to do good in obedience to his commandments.

In other words, having restored us to fellowship with himself and given us new life in Jesus Christ, God did not then just leave us to our own devices—wandering around in the desert, wondering what to do, making up the rules as we go along. No. By means of his commandments, God provides instruction and guidance. God shows us the way. He gives us *torah,* which means he "points the finger." "This is the way," he says to us. "Walk in it, that you may have life and have it more abundantly." We pray in the Lord's Prayer, "Lead us not into temptation," and by his commandments, God answers this petition.

Thus God's command, "You shall not kill," is a gift out of his merciful grace that instructs us how to walk in the new life in Christ with respect to the problem of abortion. Indeed, when we consider the theological reasons behind this command, we can see that it and many of its surrounding commandments are directly applicable to the issue of abortion. "You shall have no other gods before me" (including your self and your claim that your body is your own). "You shall not kill" (your unborn child). "You shall not commit adultery" (which will destroy the home of your child and may even lead you to have an abortion). "You shall not steal" (the unborn child who belongs to God). "You shall not covet your neighbor's wife" (which can lead you into sexual sin and abortion). (See Exodus 20:3, 13-15, 17.)

The church in our promiscuous society has hesitated to press these gracious claims of God with respect to sexual sin and its corrupting results, including abortion. The courage that we found during the Civil Rights movement—which led us to triumph through sit-ins and legislative battles and in spite of murders—has crumbled before the onslaught of the sexual revolution. Of late and far too often, the American church has joined in the hedonism of a society far from God. As a result, the majority of abortions in this country are now obtained by white women who are under the age of twenty-five, have never been married, and have never had a child. And 36 million unborn children have become the victims of our cowardice.

The Goal of the Sermon: New Life in Christ

If we will not proclaim the commandments of God with respect to sex and abortion, then we also cannot proclaim the heart of the gospel—that forgiveness, healing, and new life are available through the Cross and Resurrection of Jesus Christ for us sinners. If there is no sin, there is no need of forgiveness, and Christ died in vain; and we preachers might as well forget the whole task of the pulpit and go sell insurance or do something else that is useful. If there is no sin, we can let therapy take care of the false sense of guilt under which some people labor. If there is no sin, we can believe that God condemns no one, and that we are all okay and accepted, just as we are—case closed.

However, our congregations know that they are not okay. The adulterous husband knows he has destroyed all trust in his marriage. The promiscuous teenager fears that she is heading for a catastrophe called AIDS. The woman just out of the abortion clinic has the vague sense that she may have murdered someone. The date-rapist wonders what happened to his self-respect in his lust for power. And it is the Church's business, through its preachers, to speak of those sins in order that God through his Son may deal with them.

Let me cite an example. A pastor, who is also a friend, tells the story of a woman who had undergone an abortion and who, like so many who obtain abortions, became deeply troubled by what she had done. She sought help from a counseling center and from various friends, but they only made excuses for her act and left her burdened with her guilt. Finally, she turned to the pastor of a local church and told him of her unease. "You have done wrong," he said to her, to which she replied in relief and tears, "*That's* what I wanted to hear!" At that point, repentance took place, and she could receive the forgiveness of the gospel. Until someone clearly annunciated that the woman had done wrong, healing could not begin.

We do not help our people by overlooking or denying sin. Rather, we leave them victims of guilt, with no way for their shattered relations with God to be healed by his merciful forgiveness, with no way for their old lives to be transformed by God's grace and made new.

Strategies for the Preacher

Because abortion is such a pressing problem in our time, and because it is increasingly being sanctioned and aided by both government and society, it would seem wise for the preacher to devote an entire sermon to the issue at least once a year. Sanctity of Life Sunday rolls around every year during January and furnishes an opportunity for the preacher to devote a sermon to the problem. Certainly much of the discussion above can aid the preacher in filling in the content of the sermon. In addition, there are many books devoted to the issue.

Abortion should be mentioned in other sermons as well, in conjunction with other illustrative material. For example, when the preacher is discussing the people's obligations to love their neighbors and to aid the poor and helpless, certainly our obligation to the most helpless among us, the unborn child, should be included. When the preacher is dealing with the doctrines of creation, redemption, and the Church, abortion can figure into the sermon. When the sermon is addressing our sinful attempts to be our own gods and goddesses, our propensity to take matters of life and death into our own hands by means of abortion can be cited. And perhaps most important, when the healing and forgiveness of God by means of the Cross and Resurrection are being proclaimed, that mercy should also be extended to those in the congregation who have sinned by aiding or obtaining abortions.

The sin of abortion is very real. In our day it is dismembering, scraping, and sucking out from the womb the lives of millions of children—children whom God created and who belong to him, children for whom Christ died that they might have life and have it more abundantly, children for whom God intended a place in his ongoing purpose, children whom the church is asked to lead and nurture into glorifying and enjoying God forever.

We are preachers and people in the Church of a resurrected Lord, a Lord who willed life for us—not the death of an abortion clinic. That wanton slaughter is almost unspeakable in our time, but speak to it from our pulpits we must. For we preachers have been given the task of speaking always about the God of life and the gospel of life.

Elizabeth Achtemeier is an adjunct professor of Bible and homiletics at Union Theological Seminary in Richmond, Virginia. She is the author of many theological articles and books. Most recently, with Terry Schlossberg (see her sermon below), Dr. Achtemeier coauthored Not My Own: Abortion and the Marks of the Church *(Grand Rapids: Eerdmans, 1995). A version of this essay first appeared in the January–February 1996 issue of* Preaching.

Chapter 2
The Mother of All Battles

Connie Roland Alt

SCRIPTURE LESSONS
Old Testament: Isaiah 44:24-28; 45:8-12; 46:3-4
Epistle: Ephesians 6:10-20
Gospel: John 8:31-46

OPENING PRAYER
Ephesians 6:19-20

O h, how I have struggled with this sermon! So much to say, so little time. Such a vast and boundless ocean of misery. Such a daunting struggle to save one more, tiny, fragile child of God.
When the preacher works with the lectionary readings, the preacher has boundaries. There are many things you can say, but only a few you should say. At your best, you listen to God's Word and Spirit and then offer the one thing needful. And I hope that the one thing we have heard from Paul's Letter to the Ephesians is a burning desire to defend the little ones with the whole armor of God.

I realize that this morning I am preaching to the choir. Most of you know what abortion is and does. Most of you are outraged at the slaughter of the innocents that continues unabated. Most of you know The United Methodist Church's official position on abortion: our denomination pays lip service to the sanctity of human life while we support the Religious Coalition for Abortion Rights (now named the Religious Coalition for Reproductive Choice) and preach a pro-choice rhetoric.

To Care or Not to Care

Do you know Calvin and Hobbes? They are comic strip characters who often speak the truth in ways that convict me. In one strip, that incorrigible little boy named Calvin is strolling and philosophizing with his pet tiger, Hobbes. "I've decided to stop caring about things," says Calvin. "If you care, you just get disappointed all the time. If you *don't* care, nothing matters, so you're never upset. From now on, my rallying cry is '**So what?!**' "

Replies Hobbes: "That's a tough cry to rally around."

And then Calvin answers: "So what?!"

I don't have to tell you how grave the situation is. President Bill Clinton, who claims that only with God's help can the nation prosper, has let it be known very clearly that he has no idea what a human being is. He has demonstrated not a guilelessness, but a naive gullibility. He has shown an intolerance for a truly diversified America that guarantees freedom and justice for all.

We have news for you, Mr. President: This country is in for the Mother of All Battles. "For we are not contending against flesh and blood, but against the principalities, against the powers, against the world rulers of this present darkness, against the spiritual hosts of wickedness in the heavenly places" (Eph. 6:12).

We are battling the father of lies. And for whatever reason, many leaders of our denomination have exchanged the truth for a lie. With Falstaff, in Shakespeare's *Henry IV*, we say, "Lord, Lord, how this world is given to lying." And we are surrounded by fellow believers— good, well-intentioned Christians—who have been hoodwinked.

The Lie

What is the lie that we rebuke, here, today? The lie is the claim that babies confined to their mothers' wombs are not human, not persons. And even if they are, so says the lie, many are worthless. All the attendant lies that embroider this cloth with ugly colors and chaotic stitching do not alter abortion's status as a hopeless, desperate act that is morally bankrupt.

When I was a child, the term *pregnant* was considered vulgar. My mother never allowed me to say it. In respectable company you could say that a woman was "going to have a baby," or that she and her husband were "expecting a baby" or just "expecting." I even heard folks say, "She's with child." There was nothing untrue or euphemistic about those descriptions. We hoped that she would not miscarry and that the baby would be healthy. But we knew, if all went as expected, that the pregnant woman indeed would have her baby.

Pulitzer Prize–winning poet Anne Sexton's poem "The Abortion" describes the feelings of one woman after having an abortion. In my interpretation, the poem expresses the shame and grief of knowing that a baby who should have been born is gone forever. In an abortion, a baby suffers and dies.

The Horrible Truth

The harsh truth—so harsh it sounds like a lie—is that babies are bleeding to death. The harsh truth is that four thousand times a day in the United States the blood of living mothers mingles with the blood and tiny body parts of their dead children in that cold metal pan beneath those cold metal stirrups. It happens 1.6 million times a year, almost 30 million times in twenty years. The ghastly truth is that our public sewer systems are gushing with the blood and remains of tiny babies whose torn and bruised limbs and crushed skulls are run through industrial garbage disposals like scrapings from a dinner plate. The truth is that our public water systems are poisoned with innocent blood. You cannot taste it. You cannot smell it. For you see, we have cleaned it up. We have washed our hands of the crimes.

Do you know what the obscenity is? The obscenity is not that we describe the results of these crimes so graphically. Rather, it is the unrelenting charade that pretends that abortion does not do what I have just described. It is monumentally obscene that we know about it and say nothing and do nothing. One can only conclude that, in Jesus' words against the Sadducees, we "know neither the scriptures nor the power of God" (Mark 12:24).

Paul wrote, "The wrath of God is revealed from heaven against all ungodliness and wickedness of men who by their wickedness suppress the truth" (Rom. 1:18). If we are not exposing the lies and telling the truth, we are aiding and abetting the father of lies. And thousands of innocent children suffer and die each day. And women are assaulted by money-grubbing abortionists, who refuse to tell the truth because they would lose business. And men lose their children, grandparents lose their grandchildren. Children lose brothers and sisters. Parents lose their authority. We all lose community and hope. Yet some still claim that there is no death here. And we are all silent cowards. Silent. Silent as the grave.

This Is a Call to Arms

Today is a call to arms, my sisters and brothers. A call to arms in a peaceable kingdom where "we are more than conquerors through him who loved us" (Rom. 8:37). A call to stand firm (Eph. 6:13). Proverbs 14:25 says, "A truthful witness saves lives, / but one who utters lies is a betrayer." And the psalmist reminds us that in the midst of the battle God's "faithfulness is a shield and buckler" (Ps. 91:4).

Today is a call to arms. Actually, the Mother of All Battles was won by Jesus Christ on the Cross on D-Day, on deliverance day. But the day of total victory, V-Day, is still ahead. The Great War over sin and death has been fought and won, though this battle still rages. In the meantime, with renewed energy and courage, we will take up the cause of defending the weakest, most vulnerable of God's children. It is not easy. We seem to be outnumbered.

But our denomination needs to hear the truth from each of us. We have to say it and pray it, again and again. We are fearfully and wonderfully made in the image of the God who sees us, loves us, and sent his Son to die for us so that we might have boundless hope. Persevere. Expose the lies. Preach the truth. Remember Dr. Martin Luther King, Jr., who asked and answered: "How long? Not long. Because a lie cannot live forever."

In his famous letter from a Birmingham, Alabama, jailhouse, Dr. King wrote that "injustice anywhere is a threat to justice everywhere." We, as United Methodists, know that as well as we know the first verse of "O For a Thousand Tongues to Sing." It is time—right now—that "justice [for our littlest ones] roll down like waters, and righteousness [in our church] like an everflowing stream" (Amos 5:24).

Finally, fellow United Methodists, I believe, as Mahatma Gandhi once said, that "nonviolence and truth are inseparable and presuppose one another."

This is a call to arms.

Arms for holding the unwanted and the unloved.

Arms for hugging and comforting women who have had abortions, and offering them the peace and forgiveness that only our Lord and Savior Jesus Christ can offer.

Arms for protecting and shielding the helpless and oppressed.

Arms for linking together in unity of purpose for declaring the truth.

Arms to lift up holy hands in supplication and constant prayer for a stop to the lies that perpetuate the atrocity of abortion.

Arms that reach out the helping hands of a truly warmhearted people dedicated to scriptural holiness and reforming the nation in the name of our Lord.

This is a call to loving arms. To God be the glory!

Connie Roland Alt is the pastor of Christ United Methodist Church in Wilmington, Delaware. This sermon was first delivered on January 22, 1993, at a worship service at Simpson Memorial Chapel, in The United Methodist Building, Washington, D.C.

Chapter 3
Rejoicing in the Truth

John B. Brown

SCRIPTURE LESSONS
  Old Testament: Nehemiah 8:1-4a, 5-6, 8-10
  Epistle: 1 Corinthians 12:12-30
  Gospel: Luke 4:14-21

I n the fall of 1981, a professor from Temple University made his way to Vermont, to a little village near where my family and I were then living. The purpose of his visit was to deliver an installment sermon for a younger friend who was beginning a new pastorate. The professor was the Reverend Franklin Littell, a scholar of the Jewish Holocaust.

Littell began his sermon with an article from a recent newspaper that described how increasing noise levels in American society are contributing to the loss of hearing in our children. The article stated that many children today are, as a result of this increasing noise, becoming more and more tone-deaf.

Certainly, such tone deafness is a serious enough matter. However, Professor Littell went on to say that far more serious than physical tone-deafness in children is the spiritual and moral tone-deafness that riddles many of our children. All too often, claimed Littell, our children cannot tell the difference between right and wrong, good and evil, truth and falsehood.

Professor Littell's was a most memorable sermon. I have thought about it many times. Recently it came to mind again as I read the texts for today, the Third Sunday of Epiphany, and as I reflected on the fact that today, this very day, is the sixteenth anniversary of the United States Supreme Court's infamous *Roe v. Wade* decision. *Roe v. Wade*, of course, struck down all state abortion law and, in effect, legalized abortion on demand in America. The results have been over 20 million abortions—the destruction of 20 million children. Sadly, the decision has also meant that over 15 million women have become the second victim of abortion; many of them, if not most, struggle with the sadness, pain, and guilt of their act to this very hour.

Should there be any of these women or their relatives here this morning, I invite you to come and talk with me or with one of the other pastors of our church. If need be, we will find another woman who has gone through this experience to talk with you. God's grace is available to you. All of us—men as well as women, young as well as old—need divine grace. All of us need a Savior. And we have one: the Savior of the world, Jesus Christ.

Turning from God, Distorting the Truth

But how have these millions of abortions come to pass? And with them, how have growing numbers of infanticides come to pass? And how have increasing numbers of cases of active euthanasia (in which a sick person is not merely allowed to die but is actively put to death) come to pass? How?

I believe that the abortions, the infanticides, and the cases of active euthanasia of this time and place can be traced to the insight of that Vermont sermon: A growing number of men and women in our society—including many leaders in academia, politics, business, the entertainment industry, and the national media—have become spiritually and morally tone-deaf. They can no longer, they will no longer, recognize spiritual and moral truth. Sadly, this includes many leaders in our churches and seminaries.

Psalm 19, this morning's call to worship, states that

> The law of the LORD is perfect,
>   reviving the soul;
> the testimony of the Lord is sure,
>   making wise the simple;
> the precepts of the LORD are right,

rejoicing the heart;
the commandment of the LORD is pure,
    enlightening the eyes . . .
the ordinances of the LORD are true,
    and righteous altogether. . . .
Moreover by them is thy servant warned;
    in keeping them there is great reward.
But who can discern his errors?
    Clear thou me from hidden faults.
Keep back thy servant also from presumptuous sins;
    let them not have dominion over me!
Then I shall be blameless,
    and innocent of great transgression. (Ps. 19:7-8, 9*b*, 11-13)

When the truth of this psalm is enthroned in our hearts and minds, we are in communion with God. It is then that we are able to tell right from wrong, good from evil, justice from injustice.

How is it that the Word of the Lord, the law and commandments of the Lord, have not been heeded? How is it that God's Word—especially with regard to the issue of abortion—has been ignored?

There are many reasons, were the whole story to be told. There is the desire that many people have for freedom without responsibility. There is the sexual revolution. There is the push for a radical, ideological form of women's liberation. There is the secularization of our society. And there is the secularization of the churches. But certainly one of the primary contributing factors has been the deliberate distortion of the truth.

Truth can be distorted in a number of ways. One way truth is distorted is through the deliberate telling of lies. Dr. Bernard N. Nathanson is now a pro-life physician. However, just sixteen years ago he was a strong pro-choice activist and the director of one of the nation's largest abortion clinics. His pro-choice activism and practice ended after he became convinced of the humanity of the unborn child through his research in fetology. In *Aborting America*, Nathanson and coauthor Richard N. Ostling admit that many of the statistics concerning the number of deaths from illegal abortions, which Nathanson and his pro-choice cohorts employed, were pure fabrications. Nathanson and others in the National Abortion Rights Action League (NARAL) and its forerunner organization deliberately inflated the number of illegal abortions for one sole purpose: to manipulate legislators and politicians into supporting abortion on demand.[1]

The Euphemistic Temptation

Another widely used method of distorting the truth is the corruption of the language used to describe abortion. Consider the use of euphemisms. A euphemism is a mild and inoffensive expression that is substituted for another expression that is considered too harsh. For example, we use the statement, "he has passed away," as a euphemism for the statement, "he died."

The use of euphemisms can even be humorous. For instance, while delivering a speech on agricultural affairs, former president Harry S. Truman used the word *manure.* Following his talk, a highly indignant woman from the audience approached and spoke with Mrs. Truman. "It's just not proper," said the woman, "for the President of the United States to use such a word as *manure* in public. Couldn't you get him to use a better word, a less offensive word, like *fertilizer?*" To which Mrs. Truman replied, "What you don't realize is that it took me twenty years to get him to use the word *manure!*"

Slang expressions intensify language, but euphemisms soften language. Sometimes euphemisms go further and actually distort what is being communicated. This is particularly the case when someone wants to cover up something that is evil and immoral, such as abortion. As the old Yiddish proverb puts it, "The truth can walk around naked, only lies must be clothed in euphemism." A euphemism becomes evil when it is used to distort and deceive, when the person using it no longer heeds the powerful words about truth in Psalm 19, when the person using it no longer heeds the truth of God's law preserving his people from presumptuous sins.

Often with regard to abortion, euphemisms are used in place of the word *abortion* and the phrase *unborn child. Abortion,* in the pro-choice vocabulary, becomes *cleaning out of the uterus, emptying of the uterus,* or *termination of pregnancy.* Likewise, *unborn child* becomes *fetus* (used in a pejorative sense), *garbage, parasite, product of conception, protoplasmic mass,* or *subhuman piece of tissue.* Considering these substitutions, you can easily see that the purpose behind their usage is distortion and deception. They are used to cover up what is in fact taking place in abortion: the destruction of a child, the destruction of over 20 million children who were created in the image and likeness of God. You see, the perversion of language undermines the truth so that the evil of abortion may easily follow. The perversion of language also occurs so that infanticide and euthanasia may follow: in both cases, the word *vegetable* is used to describe a disabled, ill, injured, comatose, or dying person; then the so-called vegetable can be dispatched at will.

The truth is, every human being—no matter how young, no matter how helpless—is a human being. The truth is, every human being is created by God, through the natural workings of conception. The truth is, every human being is one for whom Christ died. Therefore, every human being is worthy of our respect.

We know from the Word of God that every human being—whether independent or dependent, healthy or injured, mobile or comatose—is a human being worthy of respect. The Word of God, not science, is our rule. The Word of God is truth, truth revealed by God, truth that sometimes eludes the calculations and measurements of science. Through the Word of God, we learn who God is and what he is like; and we learn who human beings are and how they are to be treated.

In their book, *Whatever Happened to the Human Race,* Francis A. Schaeffer and C. Everett Koop write that

> people are special and human life is sacred, whether or not we admit it. Every life is precious and worthwhile in itself—not only to us human beings but also to God. Every person is worth fighting for, regardless of whether he is young or old, sick or well, child or adult, born or unborn, or brown, red, yellow, black or white.[2]

Which Truth?

Professor Littell, concluding his memorable sermon, asked this question: How do we know what the truth is? How are we able to tell the difference between right and wrong? How are we to enter communion with God and his truth? In dealing with such important issues as abortion, infanticide, and euthanasia, how are we to know what is right? The answer Franklin Littell gave that day is the answer I offer today: follow the lead of the Bible, the revealed Word of God, our only rule of faith and practice. Professor Littell pointed specifically to the

Torah, the first five books of the Bible. It is there, and in the person and teaching of Jesus, said Littell, that we find those great principles and narratives that sketch righteous living.

This is the very point of today's lesson from Nehemiah. The story of Nehemiah and Ezra is one of the great stories of reformation in the Old Testament. The Jewish people had been exiled as a result of the Lord's judgment on their sins—sins of oppression, idolatry, and injustice—sins every bit as grave as those of our time. An important, vital part of that reformation was the rediscovery of the Law of God, and the renewing of the covenant of the people on the basis of God's Law.

After hearing the Law read in public, the people of God rejoiced in the Lord, in his Law, and in his truth. Once again they knew who they were and to whom they belonged. Once again they had a basis for distinguishing good from evil, true worship from idolatry, justice from injustice. Once again they could experience God's forgiveness.

In our hands we now have the very same Law and truth of God. Indeed, not only the Law but also the gospel, the good news about Jesus the Christ.

In remembering that Jesus was tortured, betrayed, and killed, we see just how evil and wrongheaded human beings can be. In Jesus' willingness to die for human beings and to forgive us, we see how good and gracious God is, how important and precious human beings are to him, and how important all our neighbors are to us.

It is in our union with Jesus Christ in faith and obedience, in Spirit and in truth, that our spiritual and moral tone-deafness is removed. In our life in and with the Holy Spirit we are enabled to hear, understand, trust, and obey God's Word. Only by following the Word of God and its truth about who human beings are will Christians bring a halt to the scourge of legalized abortion in the United States.

Truthful Practice

Several years ago a number of men, women, and children from local churches met in front of one of our local hospitals to pray and to protest against the abortions that were then being performed there. Many from our congregation were present. On that day and many others over the year and a half that followed, there were candlelight vigils, sidewalk demonstrations, and much prayer. Week by week by week, summer, winter, and spring, these activities continued. They continued until last summer, when the local paper announced that abortions would no longer be performed at this local hospital. The protests had been effective, many prayers had been answered, and many lives were spared. All because the truth of God's Word about the worth of unborn human beings had been put into practice. The truth of God, which had inspired the efforts of all those who had taken part in this effort, had prevailed.

In the truth of God's Word is our salvation, our freedom, and freedom for all people. Rejoice in him and his Word!

John B. Brown is a pastor at the Shepherd of the Hills United Church of Christ in Bechtelsville, Pennsylvania. He is also the president of the United Church of Christ Friends for Life, and served as the president of the National Pro-life Religious Council (NPRC). The above sermon was first preached at Shepherd of the Hills United Church of Christ on January 22, 1989.

Chapter 4
The Source
of Human Dignity

Paul M. Clark

Brothers and sisters in Christ, hear the Word of the Lord according to Jeremiah 1:5, "Before I formed you in the womb I knew you, / and before you were born I consecrated you."

Meeting on May 28, 1993, the highest court in Germany struck down previous abortion laws on the grounds that they were not sufficiently protective of unborn life. The court based its claim on a post–World War II constitutional clause which states that "human dignity is inviolable." That phrase appears in the constitution of a country shaken by war and left in a state of shock when the atrocities committed by the Nazi regime were openly revealed. The claim that "human dignity is inviolable" gives us much to consider as we ponder our time and our place. We might well ask, to put it bluntly: What has happened to human dignity? Where has it gone? Where do we find it? And why do we need it?

What is dignity? It is a word not often used in popular culture. To some, it smacks of royalty, of hierarchy. The word *dignity* comes from the Latin word *dignitas*, which means "work" or "merit." The dignity of which we are speaking is that of a human being who is the work of God, who is created by God, who is worth something to God, who will have the chance to live because God, the good Creator, bestows life. Human life has dignity because it has great worth. Life's worth is not based on what we do or on the value we assign to it. Life has great worth because God has created, given, and sustained it. And God's work is inviolable, not open to violation. That is the basis for human dignity.

Where Is Dignity?

What has happened to human dignity? In our society the essential dignity of the human being has been lost, or it is at least being casually and frequently denied. It used to be that the primary argument of the pro-choice forces was that before birth, the embryo or fetus could not be called a human life. Some, like Whoopi Goldberg, referred to the embryo as "stuff coming together." In recent years, reasoning from medical science alone, most of the society has come to believe that human life does indeed begin at conception. But now the issue is whether that life has dignity, whether that life has intrinsic worth.

Actress Margot Kidder says, "Abortion might be killing a life. But if there is a sin, it is the sin that we adults perpetrate on the children of the earth—who truly are innocent and defenseless—by bringing those children into the world when they will not be cared for." What has happened to human dignity? Is there no worth for a child who is unwanted? Is there no worth for a child who is born with a disability or deformity? Is there no worth for a child with Down syndrome? Or, for that matter, for an old man or an old woman lying in a bed in a nursing home? No, these people have come to be viewed as burdens to society, not as gifts of life from God.

But the Scriptures record this message from God to Jeremiah: "Before I formed you in the womb I knew you, / and before you were born I consecrated you." This is dignity—to be known by God, to be created and formed by God, to be consecrated by God for active service in his name. In the book of Acts, Paul reinforces Jeremiah's message and reminds the Church that our God, "The God who made the world and everything in it, being Lord of heaven and earth, does not live in shrines made by man, nor is he served by human hands, as though he needed anything, since he himself gives to all men life and breath and everything" (Acts 17:24-25).

Yet what has happened to human dignity? It has been lost because God has been lost. It has been tossed away with other "useless things" by "the enlightened." They have tossed away absolute truth, objective morality, the Ten Commandments. If life is but a series of mutations and evolutionary jumps from the slimy organisms of a primal sea, then maybe it is not important to protect human life. Then maybe it is not important to have a government that protects its citizens—all its citizens. But if we believe that life is a gift of the Creator, that he created humankind for a purpose, then there is inherent in that gift of life—whether newly conceived, suffering, aged, or near death—dignity and inestimable worth.

But in the darkness of this world, the voices rage on. Voices against life. Voices against the dignity of life. Actually, and sometimes unknowingly, they are voices for death. And in our society, we see death more and more often. Its frequency overwhelms us. We get lost in the body count. Emerson wrote these poetic lines:

> The south wind brings life, sunshine and desire
> And on every mountain meadow breathes aromatic fire.
> But over the dead, he has no power.
> The lost, the lost he cannot restore.
> And looking over the hills I mourn
> The darling who shall not return.[1]

The little ones killed by abortion are lost. Short of the Kingdom come, their lives cannot be restored in this world. Theirs could have been lives of hopes and dreams. Their lives may not have had the best of circumstances. They may not have had all the things that we have. Nevertheless, their lives were given by God. And who knows what blessings they might have been to others and to us?

But they are lost, and we cannot look over the hills to see their graves, for they are not even given the decency of an ordinary burial. It appears as though America has lost the meaning of dignity. Or has it? Is it too late? As long as this nation stands, as long as our world endures, as long as you and I make our words and convictions known, as long as there are those who will stand for justice, and as long as God continues to rule all things and push all things toward that great day of reckoning, then it is not too late. Right now, God is in heaven, the earth is still rotating, and we are here, so there is still time. But perhaps not much. For God lets a nation defying his laws go only so long before he judges it. There is a limit to what God allows.

The American people need to realize that behind what they read and hear in the newspapers and on the television and radio, behind the abortion rights slogans (especially the infamous phrase, "right to choose"), behind the very sound of a word such as *choice,* there lurk dragons. The Scriptures tell us much about that old, evil foe who desires our destruction. It is the devil and his constant temptation to evil that seeks to turn upside-down God's good creation, including the dignity of life itself.

The Origins of Dignity

Where, then, do we find dignity? How can we regain it? We find it in the one who had it in the first place, in God. The dignity of human life is derived from our Father, our Creator. Therefore, to deny our dignity and worth is to deny the dignity and worth of God himself.

The sacredness of human life was lifted up when God himself came down in the flesh, in Jesus Christ. In Jesus Christ was life, and that life was the light of the world. He was the One sent to save us from our sins. Now, every life conceived should have the opportunity not only to have life itself, but to encounter and receive this Savior and Lord, this God who came down on our behalf, this God who died on the Cross for our sins and who rose from the dead that we might have life—here and now, and life hereafter, with him.

Christ died for all—for the youngest and for the oldest and for those in between. If we would search for dignity, we will find it here in the Savior and in his life. In his earthly life he clearly showed his love for all humankind. Remember when he was preaching, and the disciples were asking him to send away those pesky children? Like many of us on occasion, these disciples wanted to send away the children. We can imagine that the disciples wanted to hear, without interruption, the teaching of Jesus. The children must have been making noise. They must have been creating distractions. Maybe one had pulled the hair of another, and others might have been rolling around in the dirt the way children often do. And so the disciples cried out, "Master, send them away!" But Jesus welcomed the children—helpless, small, vulnerable, dependent, little children—and said, "Let the children come to me, and do not hinder them; for to such belongs the kingdom of heaven" (Matt. 19:14). Jesus took the ones that the strong had pushed to the fringes and margins of society; he placed them at the center and thereby restored the children's dignity. Those children, and all children, are the Savior's children.

But so often today's voices sound even worse than those of the first disciples. "We don't want more welfare children," it is said. "An unwanted child is better off aborted." "My life is where I want it to be; a child would only mess things up." And on and on. How can any of us look a little child in the eye—your child, your grandchild, any child—and try to explain the "right to choose," the right to eliminate a child because the parents do not want him or her?

What Can We Do?

Behind it all lurks the question, What can we do? We know and we confess that every human life has worth, that life is from God and that the taking of innocent life is killing and the breaking of the Fifth Commandment. But for many, abortion is simply the "right to choose." Abortion is simply "death with dignity" for the youngest and littlest. But what is dignity? Dignity recognizes the worth of human life. Dignity stems from a deep appreciation and understanding that human life is a gift from God. There is no dignity in abortion. Abortion is simply the taking of a life deemed not worthy of living. Abortion is death deceitfully parading around as an answer to a human problem.

How do we fight against the denial of dignity in abortion? We must see that we are in the midst of a battle, sometimes subtle and sometimes not. We must fight against apathy. We must remain steadfast in our battle for human dignity. Steadfastness means that we continue to be guided by love and by our first mission of proclaiming the gospel of Jesus Christ. For the real God of this real gospel heals and changes real lives. This God can bring life out of death. Even so, we must fight a torrent of spite that rages against God. We must fight against today's obsession with self.

We must get what C. S. Lewis once called "the good infection." That is, we must be infected with the compassion for the helpless, infected with the love for the good and the right, infected to the point where we act. Certainly, we will act neither by self-righteously taking the law into our own hands nor by using the very weapons of violence that we deplore. But we will act by patiently, quietly, faithfully continuing in the toilsome work of changing minds, educating youth, helping young women with crisis pregnancies find alternatives to abortion, easing the pain of those who suffer, caring for and offering forgiveness to those who have taken life. This is work, to be sure. It is work in the trenches. It is work that is long, hard, and lacking an end in sight. But it is God's work, and we are called to participate in it.

The roar of the dragon can be deafening at times. But it need not be frightening. Truth will win over untruth. Light will win over darkness, because light has come into the world and this light dispels darkness. This light is Jesus Christ, and the victory he has won is the victory over death itself. As the Body of Jesus Christ, as the Church, we are to be light in a world of darkness. We are to be the salt of the earth. The Church's victories, our victories, will not come often or easily. Even so, we are called to be faithful, faithful to God and faithful to his holy Word, in the service of human dignity.

Paul M. Clark is the pastor of St. Paul Lutheran Church in Fowler, Michigan. His sermon was preached on January 22, 1995.

Chapter 5

Fathers, Faithfulness, and Future Generations

Edward Fehskens

SCRIPTURE LESSONS
  Old Testament: Psalm 78:1-11
  New Testament: Matthew 1:18-24

Last summer I went with my son to a Denton, Texas, stadium. We walked into the stadium, filled with thirty-five thousand men, to hear about being men of God, men of integrity. The men assembled in that stadium longed to be enabled by the grace of God to be men of God—the men we are called to be, the husbands we are called to be, the fathers we are called to be. It was a time of encouragement, but it did not last long. Looking over the prairie, we saw thunderclouds approaching. One local Texas weather "expert" joked, "That's all right. It's a couple of hours off." Fifteen minutes later, the sky fell. A Texas-size storm hit the stadium with fury. The winds started blowing, and everyone started scurrying for shelter, for cover. Lightning was striking. It was a dangerous situation, for there was no shelter, no cover, to be found.

So the thousands of men trapped in that stadium tried to cram underneath its few bleachers. At that time, it seemed that this whole experience was about to become one big washout, a big waste of time and money. But as I stood under that stadium with my son and all those other men, getting soaked to the bone, I thought, "This is what has gone wrong with our country, our churches, and our families. Our nation has lost its covering. Our churches suffer from a loss of covering. And our families, in too many instances, have lost their covering. Why? Because men of God are absent. Too many men—men of integrity; men who have committed their hearts, their minds, and their lives to the absolutes of God's Word and have been integrated into the truth; men who live for Jesus Christ and his Church; men who can weather the dangers, the hardships, and the persecution that come their way; men who count suffering as nothing compared to the joy of taking up the cross; men who are striving to live lives of holy obedience to him—are absent."

So, men, I want to talk to you, but I hope that you women will also appreciate this word. All of us need to think about men of God standing up and about how their standing up connects with life issues.

The Storm Against Life

A storm has swept over our nation. It is a dangerous storm. It brings lightning of a kind: violence and death. There are mothers killing their own children. There are abortion clinics located across the street from school playgrounds. There is child pornography. There are children who do not know their fathers.

Consider the following U.S. statistics:

• 1.1 million children are born out-of-wedlock each year; that is nearly 30 percent of all births.[1]

• 22 percent of all white children and 67 percent of all black children were born to single mothers in 1991; the trend among white teens is tending toward the experience of black teens, so this is a moral problem, not a racial issue.[2]

• 26 percent of all children born can be classified as "illegitimate," which is not a put-down but an accurate description of a home without a father, and the trend is increasing.[3]

• 1 million children per year go through the divorce or separation of their parents.[4]

• "About 60 percent of children born in the 1990s will not spend their whole childhood with their fathers." [5]

• 50 percent of today's children are likely to live in a single-parent family before adulthood.[6]

These are the statistics; this is a snapshot of what happens when men abandon women and children. For when men abandon their God-given roles, women and children are the ones who really suffer. Therefore, it is time for men to stand up and take their rightful places in marriage and family. If, by God's grace, we men will stand up, if we will become stronger husbands and fathers, we will advance the cause of protecting vulnerable lives in this society.

A Men's Issue

I will never forget a conversation about abortion I had with an executive leader of one of the largest Lutheran denominations in the United States. After I had made a brief presentation, the woman asked me, "What does this have to do with you, since you are a man?" I responded, "It has everything to do with me, because I am a man, a husband, and a father. Because I have a wife and children—and, not incidentally, because abortion is wrong—I have to say something about it. Indeed, I have to do something about it, if I am to be faithful to God."

In an excellent article, "Abortion: A Men's Issue," author Gary Thomas stated that "Abortion remains legal in this country largely because men are willing to allow it. A national ministry surveyed women who had aborted one or more children, and found that 91 percent of them would not have chosen an abortion if a viable and realistic alternative could have been found."[7] That is survey language, but it means that a vast majority of the women who choose abortion would choose otherwise—if men would stand by them and give them a viable alternative, if men would stand steady and take responsibility for their behavior, if men would stand true and shoulder the obligations of fatherhood.

Male irresponsibility translates into aborted babies. When a man says, "It's a women's issue," he abandons the mother and the little one to the abortionist. When a pastor says, "It's a political issue," he abandons the mother and her unborn child to the abortionist. When a father says, "It's a respectability issue," he abandons his daughter and grandchild to the abortionist.

It is time to call men to responsibility before God and before women and children. Here, Jesus is the model. Our Lord was always moved with compassion—not sentimentality—at the sight of suffering people. Likewise, we should be moved with compassion. Men should be especially moved with compassion, even as Jesus was. We men must not abandon, but must move forward to provide covering, strength, and support. It is time for men to stand up, to provide for and protect women and children.

It is insufficient to say that the feminist movement or the United States Supreme Court has stripped men of their rights, though there is some truth in that statement. For if a woman chooses to abort, the father of the unborn has no rights—none whatsoever—to protect the life of his unborn child. Even so, it is insufficient to blame radical feminism and American law for stripping men of their rights. For if men have been stripped of their rights, they have done it to themselves: by abandoning their responsibilities to women and children, they have abdicated their rights. Men have not been emasculated. Rather, men have emasculated themselves by turning down their husbanding and fathering responsibilities.

After we have engaged feminists in dialogue, after we have read through all the legal journals and reviews, the unborn child still cries out, "Where is my father?" The abandoned child cries into her pillow at night, "Where is my daddy?" Some of you have lived this reality and know what it is like. You know what it is like to go to bed each night and get up each morning with no father around. You know the burden, the strain, and the sorrow that his absence leaves.

Where are the men of God? Imagine with me. Imagine what our congregations would be if men truly answered the call for leadership. Imagine what could happen if men replaced apathy with action. Imagine what our communities, our school boards, and our civic organizations would be if men of principle, integrity, conviction, courage, and faith stepped up and spoke with one voice, with moral authority, as our Lord spoke. Imagine what our nation would be if men of God stepped up and said, "Enough! No More! You will not corrupt our children, or take them from us, any longer!" Imagine what the pro-life movement and our government would be if millions of men, in the boldness of truth and with righteous indignation, stepped up and said with one voice, "No more aborting our children. We will no longer allow you to hurt our mothers, our wives, our sons, our sisters, and our daughters. In the name of Jesus Christ, no more!"

Our nation does not have an abortion problem or a drug problem or a sexuality problem, so much as it has a father problem. It is time for fathers, under the direction of our heavenly Father, to step into the arena, to step into the circle of their families, to step into their marriages, and yes, to suffer if necessary, to go to the cross if necessary. We must never quit, never abandon, never run off. A man of God is a man who goes to the front line, a man who is willing to die to protect his family.

Responsible Fatherhood: Providing and Protecting

"A black father of several sons was being interviewed on television. One son was a doctor, one was a college professor, one a pastor, others in business—all successful and heading happy, productive families. When asked how, in a white-dominated society, his sons had become such a success, the man replied, 'I made them that way'."[8] In other words, he passed on those values. This father had his priorities straight in his life and in his marriage. His kids knew how to respect and treat women because they had seen how their dad had done it. They had seen how dad had treated his wife, his sweetheart, the love of his life.

Men have been called to this kind of responsibility. The health of our children's relationships stems in large part from the health of our own relationships and our own marriages. Are we men tending the most important vineyard that God has given us: our home, our marriage, our relationship with our wives and children?

Regarding the character of a bishop, 1 Timothy 3:4 states, "He must manage his own household well, keeping his children submissive and respectful in every way." This suggests that it is not the mother's job to teach the children to toe the line; instead, it is the father's responsibility. Men, our children will respect us for two reasons: first, because we live in a way that deserves respect; and second, because as men of integrity, as men of faith, we expect such respect from our children.

Matthew 1:18-25 tells us about Joseph. Joseph was the foster father of Jesus. He was a just and good man, though he was in a tough situation: Mary was pregnant, and the child she carried was not his. Therefore, he "resolved to divorce her quietly" so that she would not be subjected to scorn and possibly to stoning. But God had something else in mind for Joseph. God sent an angel to tell Joseph that Jesus was "of the Holy Spirit" and that he should take Mary as his wife. In response, Joseph did two things: he believed God, and he obeyed God. And because Joseph believed and obeyed God, Mary was protected and provided for. Since Joseph took Mary into his home, Jesus was given the protection of Mary's womb.

Later, when the wise men avoided telling Herod where he could find Jesus, Herod became very angry. So Herod ordered his soldiers to kill every male child under the age of two in the city of Bethlehem. The Church remembers this event on December 28, The Day of the Holy Innocents. An angel soon appeared and told Joseph to get up and sneak Mary and Jesus out of the country to safety. At the risk of his own life, Joseph did exactly that. As a result, Jesus' life was spared. Had he been caught by the government, Joseph would have been punished, possibly with death. But Joseph was a man of principle, a man of integrity, a man of faith and obedience, a man who fulfilled his responsibility as a provider for and protector of his family.

We might ask ourselves: Where would Jesus be without Joseph? God's plan of salvation included God's plan for Joseph. Thank God, then, not only for Mary's faith and obedience but also for Joseph's faith and obedience.

We should understand that what a man does is crucial not just for the present, not just for the here and now, not just for his present family and home. The wonderful promise of God to a righteous man is blessing from generation to generation; indeed, to the children's children the blessing will pass. Because Joseph provided and protected in faithful obedience to God, the salvation of the world was achieved, once for all, in the fulfillment of God's plan. For God did not intend that Jesus should die in the womb of Mary or under the sword of Herod; instead, God the Father intended that his Son give his life up on a cross as a ransom for many.

Responsible Fatherhood: Passing on the Faith

God expects men not only to provide and protect but also to pass on the one, true faith. Listen again to parts of today's reading from Psalm 78:

> I will open my mouth in a parable;
> > I will utter dark sayings from of old,
> things that we have heard and known,
> > that our fathers have told us. (vv. 2-3)

That does not mean that mothers are not involved, but it means that fathers have an essential responsibility in passing on the faith to the younger generations. Verse 4 continues,

> We will not hide them from their children,
> > but tell to the coming generation
> the glorious deeds of the LORD, and his might,
> > and the wonders which he has wrought.

Fathers, are we passing on the faith we have received to our children and to our children's children?

It is a tall order for men. God's expectations for us are high. However, he has given us a role model. And his name is Jesus. A song goes something like this, "I want to be just like Jesus because my son wants to be like me." This is the key. As our children see Jesus in us, and as our wives see Jesus in us—as the world sees Jesus in us, we pass the faith on to them. And the good news is that God by his grace will transform us—people who cannot transform ourselves. As we, like Joseph, believe God and take the step of obedience, God will transform us as he transforms the world. This is how Jesus trusted and obeyed his Father. Hebrews speaks of Jesus, "who for the joy that was set before him endured the cross" (12:2).

As Jesus is our role model, here are some of his characteristics that help us understand the role of Christian husbands and fathers.

• **Jesus was a man of prayer.** During his days of public ministry, he often retreated to pray. Do we pray? Do we prayerfully seek our Father's direction as we strive to become stronger fathers in the faith?

• **Jesus was a provider.** He often supplied bread and wine, fish and water, to others. At the end of his life, he made provision for his mother by entrusting her to the care of the apostle John.

• **Jesus was a protector.** He calmed the storm and endured death to save us from death.

• **Jesus was a man of compassion.** His heart was filled with compassion for all who were lost, alone, or suffering.

• **Jesus was a man of boldness.** Whether he was before Satan or the Sanhedrin, the Pharisees or Pilate, Jesus did not back away. He was full of faith, full of the Word, full of courage.

• **Jesus was a man of faithfulness, even to the point of death.**

• **Jesus was a servant.** Indeed, "the Son of man came not to be served but to serve" (Matt. 20:28).

• **Jesus was a man who loved children.** Even in a hostile environment, Jesus was not hesitant to take a child into his arms and bless the little one.

As a sinner, I fall far short of Jesus' example in my life. Of this I am very conscious. Every night, before I go to bed, I enter each of my children's rooms and do three things. First, I say, "Father, forgive me for not being the father that I should be for these kids. Help me to do better." Second, overwhelmed with gratitude, I give thanks to the Father for blessing me so abundantly with these dear children. And third, I bless my children, as they sleep, by making a sign of the cross on their foreheads: Father, Son, and Holy Spirit. I do this to each one of them, every night, because I want the Lord Jesus Christ to bless them—and their children and their children's children—every day of their lives.

May God grant this to all of us by the grace that is ours, all sufficient, freely given, through Jesus Christ. Amen.

Edward Fehskens is a former executive director of Lutherans for Life. This sermon was first preached at the national convention of Lutherans for Life, in Kansas City, Missouri, in November 1994. He is now a pastor at Holy Cross Lutheran Church in Fort Wayne, Indiana.

Chapter 6

Who Is My Neighbor?
The Right Answer to the
Wrong Question

Michael J. Gorman

SCRIPTURE LESSONS
Old Testament: Psalm 146
New Testament: Luke 10:25-37

"Who is my neighbor?" This is an apparently innocent, innocuous question. It is a very natural, human question. In fact, however, it can be a dangerous, a deadly, even a demonic question. "Who is my neighbor?" means not only "To whom am I responsible?" but also "To whom am I *not* responsible?" It asks not only "Whom must I love?" but also "From whom may I *withhold* my love?" It seeks to discern which members of the human community are worthy of my love, and which are not.

"Who is my neighbor?" is an ancient religious and legal question. Who is in, and who is out? In modern garb this question takes a more secular and philosophical form: "Who is a person?" or "Who is a person in the full sense of the word?" Who meets the test, who possesses the criteria of personhood, of "neighbor-hood," of humanity? What biological, social, psychological, or other traits must a being have in order to merit compassion?

Such questions, no matter how common as matters of theological and philosophical and legal speculation, can indeed yield deadly results. In our country there was a time when African Americans were not considered persons by some. They did not pass the test or meet the criteria. In other countries it has been Jews or female infants or people with mental disabilities. And many of these alleged nonpersons have also been mistreated or killed without criminal charge or regret.

"Who is my neighbor?" is the wrong question. Jesus himself shows us this in Luke's brilliant account of Jesus' telling of the parable of the good Samaritan. The lawyer (an ancestor in spirit, if not flesh, of the United States Supreme Court sitting in 1973) asks, "Who is my neighbor?" (10:29), hoping to find out that he had included and excluded the right kinds of people. But by the end of the story, Jesus is asking, "[Who] proved [to be a] neighbor to the man who fell among the robbers?" (10:36). The right question is one of character, not of criteria. The right question is about *being* a neighbor, not *defining* a neighbor. And the right answer to the wrong question is very simple: Be a neighbor; be compassionate; do not be like the priest or the Levite.

What exactly was the failure of the priest and the Levite? They failed to love. They failed to recognize a neighbor. They failed ultimately to *be* a neighbor. They failed to take the side of a victim. They failed to hear a human life calling them, a person in need, a person to love. They chose the less morally demanding action, in favor of death, not life. They presumed—perhaps unconsciously, but still they presumed—that the man was not alive or was not important and therefore had no claim on them.

By acting as he did, the Samaritan gave the right response to the wrong question. *The Samaritan made a neighbor out of a question mark.* He did not assume that human life was absent; he assumed human life was present. He did not engage in philosophical or theological deliberation; he recognized a victim, a neighbor. That filled him with compassion, a compassion that led to action, to sacrifice. He did not ask, "Who is my neighbor?"; he asked, "How can I be a neighbor?"

With this parable, Jesus teaches us that "Who is my neighbor?" is the wrong question. Nevertheless, by changing the question, Jesus actually answers the lawyer's original, misguided question. To the misguided question, "Who is my neighbor?" Jesus answers, the victim is my neighbor. The one in need, the one in pain is my neighbor. The one without protection and defense is my neighbor. And why is this so? Because these are the Lord's neighbors. That is what Psalm 146 is all about.

The Lord "executes justice for the oppressed . . . gives food to the hungry . . . sets the prisoners free . . . opens the eyes of the blind . . . lifts up those who are bowed down . . . watches over the sojourners . . . upholds the widow and the fatherless" (Ps. 146:7-9). If we, as Christians, care about our neighbors, it is because first of all the Lord cares. The Lord both declares who our neighbors are and defines what it means to be a neighbor to them.

So far, I have said nothing specifically about abortion. Even so, I trust that the implications are clear. "Is the fetus a person in the full sense of the word?" is the wrong question. The right question is, "How can we, the Church, be neighbors to women and teens and families in difficult pregnancies that tempt them to consider abortion?" As we show compassion and uphold the downtrodden in the middle of their predicaments, we *become* the right answer to the wrong question. We presume in favor of life—the life of the woman and the life of the child in her womb.

As Jesus teaches us in the parable, in being a neighbor, we also answer the wrong question head-on. In every potential abortion there are at least two neighbors, two in need, two possible victims: a woman and a child, a Mary and a Jesus.

Today, some parts of the Church and some parts of society pretend there is only one neighbor in potential abortion situations: either the woman or the child. That is the wrong answer. We must have a both/and response, not an either/or response. The Church, like the good Samaritan, must learn to recognize neighbors in both the woman and the child, and to be a neighbor to each. Like the Samaritan, we may be outnumbered two-to-one—and perhaps worse—by those who side either with the woman or with the child alone. But there is a solid core of "both/and" Christians and churches. It is time for action, for Samaritan action.

Today we bear witness, inside this sanctuary and outside, through this service of worship and through another march for life. We bear witness to preachers and to parishioners and to princes. Tomorrow, however, the real work begins: convincing the churches to be the Church, and then actually being the Church. As the psalmist tells us, the oppressed—including the unborn and their mothers—are not to put their "trust in princes" or in mortals (146:3). But they should be able to place their trust in the Samaritan—in the people of God, in the Church, in us.

We are called, not to define who our neighbors are, but to be neighbors. Since the first century we Christians have said that women in need and unborn children are our neighbors. It is now time for us to *be* neighbors. That is how we will become the right answer to the wrong question—even as we continue to say, "The unborn child is our neighbor, and the woman in need is our neighbor."

*Michael J. **Gorman** preached this sermon on January 21, 1994, in the Simpson Memorial Chapel of The United Methodist Building, Washington, D.C. Currently, he is an associate professor of New Testament and the dean of the Ecumenical Institute of Theology, St. Mary's Seminary and University, Baltimore, Maryland.*

Chapter 7
The Religion of the Sovereign Self

Richard John Neuhaus

Today I intend to speak in tones of hope. Today I invoke the vision of a new day dawning, of a better day, of a day that pushes back the encroaching culture of death, of a day that holds the promise of help and hope for unborn children in peril, for women in desperation, for a nation in conflict with the truths by which it was conceived and to which it was dedicated. So understand my remarks as a testament of hope, of hope that is the posture of faith toward the future, of hope that is the persistence of love in defiance of all odds. "So faith, hope, love abide, these three; but the greatest of these is love" (1 Cor. 13:13).

The pro-life witness is a witness of love. If it ever stops being that, it will cease to claim our commitment. It is a witness motivated by love of God and by love for the neighbor whom others would exclude from the community of caring and concern. Seldom in human history have so many done so much for so long out of no rational reason other than the relentless imperative of love. When we are weary of the struggle, when we are tempted to despair, remember that to us has been given the gift—and with the gift the obligation—of sustaining amidst the darkness the luminous moment of love that is the pro-life witness.

In the past twenty years, the pro-life witness in the United States has received some mighty blows. But obviously, those blows have not been mortal. On the political and legal fronts, our opponents have triumphed again and again. But their triumph is only for a time. We have learned, if we needed to learn, the truth of the psalmist: "Put not your trust in princes" (146:3). It is understandable that some of our company are bitterly disappointed. Those who seek reasons to despair will find reasons to despair. But we have not the right to despair.

We have not the right to despair and, finally, we have not the reason to despair. We have not reason to despair if, from the very beginning, we understand that our entire struggle is premised not upon a victory to be achieved by us but upon a victory already achieved. If we understand that, far from cause for despair, we have right and reason to rejoice that we are called to such a time as this, a time of testing, a time of truth. The encroaching culture of death shall not prevail, for we know, as we read in John's Gospel, "The light shines in the darkness, and the darkness has not overcome it" (1:5). The darkness will never overcome that light. Never. Never.

Casey and the Culture War

The goal of the pro-life movement, as I understand it, is to achieve the maximum legal protection for the unborn that is politically and culturally sustainable. While most of our fellow citizens may not fully share that goal, they do want some kind of accommodation; they do want the law to encourage caring rather than license killing; they do want to give life a chance. But the faction that calls itself pro-choice will not give an inch. It deeply distrusts the American people, and with good reason. In its view, Americans are peculiarly unfit for the practice of democracy when it comes to questions that really matter. One reluctantly concludes that that contemptuous view of American democracy is now supported by a majority of the United States Supreme Court. That was made painfully clear in its 1992 decision *Planned Parenthood v. Casey*. In truth, one can claim that the questions raised by *Casey* are every bit as foundational and solemn as those pondered by Lincoln at Gettysburg.

The *Casey* decision is a decision for one side in the culture war in which America has been engaged for some time. More than politics, more than law, more than economics, the great battle in our time is for the culture. What do we mean by culture? The culture is simply the sum of the ideas by which we live; the culture is the moral air that we breathe; the culture is the habits of the heart and the behaviors of the person that form our character; the culture is communities of memory and mutual aid; the culture is the world that we would pass on to our children.

For some time now we have been engaged in a war over the culture. This is nothing less than a war over what kind of nation, what kind of people, we will be. This is not a war of our choosing. This war was declared—and it is daily and exultantly redeclared—by the proponents of myriad revolutions who presume to know better than we how we ought to live. And they do not hesitate to employ the power of government to enforce conformity to their designs. For some time now the United States has been torn into two nations: one concentrating on rights and laws, the other on rights and wrongs; one radically individualistic and dedicated to the actualized self, the other communal and invoking the common good; one viewing law as the instrument of license and the will to power, the other affirming an objective moral order by which we are obliged; one given to private satisfaction, the other to familial responsibility; one typically secular, the other typically religious; one elitist, the other respectful of the common sense of common people.

Of course this description is drawn with broad strokes. Nevertheless, it roughly describes the lines of the culture war in which we are engaged. (That reality is evident enough to anyone who attends to the increasingly ugly rancor that dominates and debases our public life.) The lines of the culture war run through the very hearts of many Americans. And as the *Casey* decision makes evident, the lines run through the Supreme Court. The five justices who made up the *Casey* majority leave no doubt about where they stand. Their decision is a clear declaration of belligerency by one side of the culture war against the other.

Casey: Triumph of the Self

Planned Parenthood v. Casey endorses the radically individualistic notion of the self-constituted self. The abortion liberty is necessary,

63

we are informed by the decision, in order "to define one's own concept of existence, of meaning, of the universe, and of the mystery of human life." I am told that, among constitutional lawyers, this is called the decision's "mystery passage." The justices wax theological about the mystery of human life in total disregard of precisely that, the mystery of human life. For the Supreme Court, the mystery of human life is to be defined by the individual; but for most of us, the mystery of human life is discovered as a gift. For the Court, authentic personhood requires freedom from an encumbering community; but for most of us, to be a person is to be a person in community.

In *Casey* the Court tells us that freedom requires freedom from family, even freedom from one's spouse. Thus it strikes down the Pennsylvania requirement that fathers be notified before mothers kill their children. To require notification, says the Court, would be an "undue burden." The only self known to this Court is the unburdened self, the autonomous self, the isolated self, the self that—in Godlike manner—defines the meaning of the universe and the mystery of life.

In *Planned Parenthood v. Casey*, unlike *Roe v. Wade*, the controlling concept is not "privacy" but "liberty"—although the end result is the same. The liberty of the Court is not what the founders of the United States called "ordered liberty," nor is it liberty directed to the good and formed by communities of care and character. According to the Court, liberty is, without remainder, the liberty of self-will, self-expression, and indeed self-creation. For this Court, that debased concept of liberty trumps every other consideration. Not to be free to choose, no matter the choice, is not to be. Obviously, the unborn, the comatose, the demented, and the senile are not free to choose. The lethal logic from *Roe* through *Casey* is that, lacking the requisites of personhood, these people should not be. The muddled language of the Court invites us to infer that, at some deeper level, these people lack being. Only the autonomous self is free to choose and therefore free to be.

When I claimed that the Court waxed theological, I did not mean it simply as a figure of speech. Although the three authors of the majority opinion—justices Kennedy, O'Connor, and Souter—seem to be blithely unaware of it, they are proposing the establishment of what might be called a state religion. Religion is commonly defined as that activity that deals with ultimate concerns. It is hard to get more ultimate than the "concept of existence, of meaning, of the universe, and of the mystery of human life." In most religions (Judaism and Christianity, for instance) the self is understood in relationship to other realities—in relationship to community, normative truth, even revelation. The court, however, recognizes no other reality than the isolated individual defining his or her own reality.

The Court reinforces the Hobbesian notion that we are a society of strangers, perhaps of enemies, and it is the chief business of the state to prevent others from interfering with or obliging the sovereign self. The *Casey* decision is a combination of statist tyranny and individualistic license. The result is the community-destroying and potentially totalitarian doctrine that society is composed of only two actors, the state and the solitary citizen. The civic religion proposed by the Court is hardly civic in character and consequence. Rather, it is the undoing of the *civitas*, of the civil society of myriad persons, associations, and communities of moral tradition interacting within the bond of civility and mutual respect.

Permit me to be entirely candid. The Supreme Court's depiction of the self, of community, and of what is meant by ultimate meaning is incompatible with Christianity, Judaism, Islam, and every tradition that espouses normative truth. Not incidentally, it is also incompatible with the lived experience of almost everybody on earth. Again, in effect, though not in name, the Supreme Court is proposing a religion. For those of us who already have a religion, the Court's religion is obviously a false religion. As distressing as this state of affairs may be, we should not be entirely surprised by it.

That New Religion and Abortion

It has been said that if you can justify abortion you can justify anything. There is a deep truth in that. If you set out to justify the attack on something so primordial, so given, so foundational to human community as a mother's love and responsibility for her child, you have to come up with a new explanation of fundamental reality, a new worldview, and finally a new religion. The Supreme Court of the United States has come up with the Religion of the Sovereign Self.

To be sure, it is not really a new religion. It is the belief to which human beings have been prone since that disastrous afternoon in the garden when humanity began its long and bloody march through history singing "I Did It My Way." The creed of the autonomous self was promulgated by the radical secularists of the Enlightenment and is still preached by their disciples today. Against that creed, the founders of this nation declared, "We hold these Truths to be self-evident, that all Men are created equal, that they are endowed by their Creator with certain unalienable Rights, that among these are Life, Liberty and the Pursuit of Happiness."

Convenience and control play a large part in the decision of justices Kennedy, O'Connor, and Souter. We are told that abortion on demand is necessary for women to "order their lives." Thus do they insult the women beyond number who believe that their lives are rightly ordered in exercising the responsibilities of marriage and motherhood. The Court assumes that the abortion license has been a critical factor, maybe the critical factor, in securing greater dignity for women. Nowhere does it note that since *Roe,* the abuse of women by irresponsible and predatory men has increased; that since *Roe,* a huge abortion industry, dominated by men, has developed and has exercised a minimum of care in extracting a maximum of profit from the suffering of women.

But women must be free to choose, says the Court, forgetting that without relevant information, without men being held accountable for their offspring, without programs that support women in childbirth and child rearing, without law that at least creates a pause before the destroying of the innocent, the choice is overwhelmingly loaded on the side of abortion. Abortion is a women's issue, says the Court, ignoring survey after survey reporting that women are more pro-life than men. Women need abortion to "order their lives," says the Court, blind to the callousness and cruelty of a society that has nothing better to say to a poor, frightened, pregnant woman than that she has a right to dispose of her own baby.

The most glaring omission in the *Casey* decision is the recognition of the other party involved in abortion. The Court says that the fetus is "potential human life" in which the state has a legitimate interest, but not a "compelling" interest that could impinge upon the unfettered right to abortion. Even the otherwise persuasive dissent by the four minority justices says that whether or not the fetus is a human life is a "value judgment." However, whether or not the fetus is a human life is not a value judgment. It is a biological and medical determination that is beyond dispute. There is absolutely no dispute that the fetus is *life*. Furthermore, since it possesses an utterly unique genetic design, it is *a* life. Finally, there is no question that this is a *human* life. Allowed to develop, the fetus will not turn out to be a goldfish.

Barring natural disaster (as in a miscarriage) or lethal intervention (as in an abortion), the little one will become what every reasonable person in the world will recognize as a human baby. The fetus is a "potential" many things—a potential rock star, a potential police officer, a potential criminal, a potential Supreme Court justice. But it is only those things potentially because it already *is* a human life. The value judgment or, more accurately, the moral judgment enters when we ask what we are going to do about this human life. What, if anything, is owed this human life? What rights, if any, are possessed by this human life? Those questions, say the dissenting four justices, are not answered by the United States Constitution; in a representative democracy, the justices continue, those questions are rightly resolved by the people. On those questions, however, the forces that call themselves pro-choice are determined not to give the people a democratic choice.

Let us put it as clearly as possible. There would be no abortion debate, there would be no pro-life movement, were it not for the two parties inescapably involved in the abortion decision: the mother and the child. In the decision to abort, the life of the deciding party may, in some rare instances be at risk. The life of the other, is always terminated. Remove the question of the other life, and there would be no dispute over abortion. The entire abortion controversy is occasioned by the perceived fact of the other life. The extraordinary thing about the Court's position is that it claims to settle the debate by ignoring the concern that occasions the debate. For this reason and others, *Casey* is wrongheaded.

As Lincoln would explain to the Stephen Douglasses of our day, *Planned Parenthood v. Casey* is not "the law of the land." It is, quite simply, one wrong decision of the United States Supreme Court affirming an earlier wrong decision of the Court (*Roe v. Wade*). And a hundred more wrong decisions will not make that earlier decision right.

We, as a country, have been this way before. Remember that at the time of the *Dred Scott* decision all three branches of government were in the hands of pro-slavery forces. Before and after he became President, Lincoln strove for the overturning of *Dred Scott*. He failed, and war came. There will not be a civil war like the last one, but the destructive effects of alienation and anger are already evident in our society as a result of law that is divorced from constitutional text, moral argument, and democratic process. As the legal interests of the Sovereign Self advance, the ever fragile bonds of civility unravel. This lawless law, that honors the Sovereign Self, invites lawlessness.

A Confident Word

We have discussed many things. Today I have no doubt tried your patience. So let me conclude with the words with which I ended my address to you eleven years ago. These words, I believe, remain as true today as they were then. And they, I believe, will be as true for the next generation that will uphold the light of life in defiance of the culture of death. I said then, "I do not know if there will again be a new birth of freedom—for the poor, the aged, the radically disabled, the unborn. But we commend our cause to the One who makes and keeps promises, to the Lord of life. In that commendation is our confidence: confidence that the long night of *Roe v. Wade* is not forever; confidence that the courts will yet be made responsible to the convictions of a democratic people; confidence, ultimately, in the dawning of a new day in which law and morality will be reconciled, in which liberty will no longer wage war on life. Let this be, then, a convention of confidence; not because we trust in our own strength but because, under God, the last word belongs not to death but to love and life—because, even now, our eyes have seen the glory of the coming of the Lord."

Richard John Neuhaus is a Roman Catholic priest, the author and editor of many books and articles on religion and society, and the editor-in-chief of First Things, *a monthly journal of religion and public life. Father Neuhaus delivered an extended version of this speech at the National Right to Life Convention on June 24, 1993.*

Chapter 8

Commemoration of the Twentieth Anniversary of *Roe v. Wade*

John Cardinal O'Connor

SCRIPTURE LESSON
New Testament: John 1:29-34

It seems to me appropriate that during this Mass, before all else, we should remind ourselves that within a handful of hours we will have a new President and Vice President of the United States. Regardless of whatever differences anyone here may have with the political, ideological, philosophical, moral, theological, or spiritual convictions of our new President and Vice President, it is surely incumbent upon us, as citizens who love our land, as Christians who are commanded to love all, to commit ourselves to prayer, to ask that our President and Vice President be inspired with the Holy Spirit to govern wisely, justly, and compassionately. It is incumbent on us, as well, to pray in a special way that the cause of human life will be enhanced during the years ahead; that everyone will be treated with dignity; and that the sacredness of every human person will be recognized in law and in fact, whether that human person is still in the womb of his or her mother, is dying of cancer, is in a wheelchair, is retarded or blind or crippled. We will pray consistently in the years ahead that *every* human person will be recognized as made in the image and likeness of Almighty God and will be supported by the government, which, as Thomas Jefferson never tired of reminding us, exists *only* for the defense of the people.

Herod v. John, Fearful v. Fearless

Today's Gospel lesson focuses on St. John the Baptist. Clearly he is considered by the Church to be a mighty figure in the Christian faith, and the bridge between the Old Testament and the New Testament. Foretelling and then actually witnessing the coming of our Divine Lord, he is the final prophet.

John the Baptist has special meaning for us today. We cannot but think of him as the man who made clear the distinction between those who live in constant fear because they trust only in themselves, and those who live without fear because of their total trust in Almighty God. Probably that which is best known about John the Baptist is his conflict with Herod Antipas (or simply Herod). Herod, who was the son of Herod the Great (who slaughtered the innocents in an effort to put the Christ Child to death), took as his wife his own sister-in-law and lived with her incestuously. When this occurred, John the Baptist, totally unafraid, singled out Herod, a man of immense power, and declared that his was unlawful conduct. To John the Baptist that was basic. He did not care what might happen to him. It was his responsibility to articulate the truth, to distinguish between good and evil, to preach what he believed he was sent to preach.

On the contrary, Herod was terrified to be so singled out. He saw John the Baptist as a major political threat. Evidence of this is from the thoroughly objective Jewish historian, Flavius Josephus, who was not one of the Scripture writers. Josephus tells us that Herod was fearful because John the Baptist was so popular with the people. Herod was afraid because John was luring so many people with his preaching. Herod was concerned that there would be a revolution, an insurrection, and that he would be overthrown. That is why Herod had John the Baptist cast into prison. And that is why, on the pretext of having made a promise to his unlawful wife, he had John beheaded.

Fear and Violence: Notes on American History

It is particularly appropriate, I think, for us to reflect on the fearful and the fearless today. For today, in a very special way, we are reminded of the sadness ushered into our society by that tragic decision of

January 22, 1973, that we refer to, often casually, as the *Roe v. Wade* decision of the United States Supreme Court.

There is another reason for reflecting on the difference between those who are fearful and those who are fearless. Tomorrow our nation officially celebrates the birthday of the Reverend Dr. Martin Luther King, Jr., who was born on a January fifteenth and assassinated on an April fourth. In thinking about the increasing meaning of Dr. King to American life, in reading more and more of his life, of his sayings, of his philosophy, of his theology, in coming to have a deeper and deeper admiration for what this man really was, I reread some things with which I have been familiar for some time.

The first of these was Jim Bishop's book *The Day Lincoln Was Shot*. In that startling book, that poignant epic, about the day that Abraham Lincoln was shot, in which every moment was of such utmost importance, the one passage that struck me most forcefully was this one, which describes the immediate reactions after the death was announced:

> Across the street from the White House, on the far side of Pennsylvania Avenue, the plain people waited to say good-by. Mostly, they were Negroes [the term used in that day] and they formed a thick dark ribbon on the walk. The cold rain stitched their backs but they did not move. The men wept too, and one called out: "If death can come to him, what will happen to us?"[1]

Violence always begets fear; and fear, in turn, begets violence. Abraham Lincoln was killed out of fear that he was going to revolutionize this country in ways that many detested. He was killed out of fear; and then, in turn, there was great fear, legitimate fear, on the part of blacks in the United States, that now they too would be hunted down. They had lost their protector. "If [this kind of violence] can come to him," they asked, "what will happen to us?"

I also turned to a book written by James Farmer, the founder of the Congress of Racial Equality, called *Lay Bare the Heart*. There Mr. Farmer writes vividly about what happened on the day that the Reverend Dr. Martin Luther King, Jr., was killed; Farmer notes that, after the shooting, he and many others were instantly rushed to cover. Fear swept the land and, as a result, so did violence. Within days subsequent to the death of Dr. King, forty-three people were killed. Violence always begets fear, and fear begets violence.[2]

Fear and Violence: Notes on the Present

The New Yorkers among us will recall what it was like during the recent summer riots in Los Angeles. There was instant fear on the streets, in the homes, of New York. People checked to make sure that their doors were locked. People who did not have to be on the streets stayed indoors. No one went outside unless compelled. The subway cars were quickly emptied. All of this was out of fear, fear that violence would very quickly ensue.

The fear-and-violence equation is a terrible equation. It is particularly terrible when we recognize that those places which were once so free from fear have now lost their security. Consider, for example, one of our finest hospitals. It is a Catholic hospital that takes care of those who are terminally ill with cancer. Acute care hospitals can do no more for these cancer patients. These special patients are beyond cure except by way of a miracle, so they go to this particular institution where they are treated with exquisite love, care, and gentleness. They are supported until the moment of death. They are given drugs to ease the pain. However, they are not given drugs that make them comatose, because it is so important for the patients to be able to relate to their families, to take care of their temporal affairs, and, most importantly, to prepare spiritually for the life to come. This is one of the most beautiful health-care facilities in the land.

How would you feel if you or a loved one were en route to that facility and learned what its medical director recently told me? He said that the major insurance carrier for this terminal-cancer facility had told him, "You are keeping people alive too long. If you continue doing this, you will lose your insurance, and you will not be able to get it anywhere else."

What security one used to have in a hospital! One went to a hospital to be treated as a patient, to be treated with gentleness, to be treated with love, to be cured if cure was possible, and to be cared for with dignity if cure was not possible. Now must we fear the potential of legislation for euthanasia or assisted suicide?

Why, in state after state, is legislation being introduced that would legalize and regulate assisted suicide? Why is such a prestigious journal as the *New England Journal of Medicine* suggesting that doctors take a new look at their responsibilities, from which one could infer that, in some circumstances, doctors can act not as agents of life but as agents of death? Why all of this?

Mother Teresa and others would tell us that much of it began on January 22, 1973, when the United States Supreme Court rendered vulnerable those who had previously been in what we thought was the safest place in the whole world—even safer than the hospital—the mother's womb. The Supreme Court decided that the unborn were no longer safe because they were not persons, not people. They were tissues; they were blobs; they were unidentifiable, undefinable. How can it be that for all of those years our country accepted the reality that the unborn have the right to life and then suddenly, by the stroke of a pen, it was declared that they are "nonpersons"—much like the *Dred Scott* decision declared blacks to be nonpersons? That was the watershed. That is when death began to assault our land. That is when we began to develop a contempt for human life. That is when we began to descend into an ethic of death, rather than raise up an ethic of life. Why? Because of fear. Herod Antipas, who had John the Baptist put to death out of fear, was the son of Herod the Great, who had all of those little babies put to death out of fear because he thought that the Christ Child had come to take his kingdom.

Casting Out Fear

Never in my life will I denounce, condemn, or even criticize a woman who has permitted her unborn baby to be put to death. Why? Because I know how many women are motivated by fear to abort their little ones: fear that they will not be able to take care of their children, fear that they will not be able to feed or support their children, fear that the children's fathers will walk out, fear that their children will be deformed or retarded, fear that they will not be able to go on to college, fear that they will lose their jobs, fear of less critical things that nevertheless seem important to them, fear that they will lose their figures, fear that whereas they wanted a boy they are going to have a girl, or vice versa. This is why I announced for the first time on October 15, 1984, and many times since then, and even if people get tired of hearing me say it, I will keep saying it and saying it again: *Any* woman, of any color, of any age, of any religion, who is pregnant and in need can come to the Archdiocese of New York, can come to me personally,

73

can call me, can come to our Catholic Charities. We will take complete care of her, free of charge. We will help her to keep her baby if she wishes to keep the baby. We will help her to have the baby adopted if that is what she wishes. We will provide medical and hospital care. We will give her the support and encouragement she needs to take away her fear.

How many young girls are fearful of what their parents might do if they learn that they are pregnant, of what their boyfriends might do, of the possibility that they might have to drop out of school? So many women, young and older, are confused and lost; but above all, they are fearful. So what happens? Fear leads to violence—the death of an unborn baby. This is why we make this unconditional offer to help.

St. John tells us that love is the one thing that drives out fear. "There is no fear in love, but perfect love casts out fear. For fear has to do with punishment, and he who fears is not perfected in love" (1 John 4:18).

As you know, we have established a new religious community, the Sisters of Life. These wonderful and, for the most part, professional women have given up everything to take care of the pregnant, to take care of the elderly, to take care of the wheelchaired, to enhance a sense of the sacredness of human life. In other words, the Sisters of Life will love people who are otherwise fearful. The Sisters of Life will not condemn them. They will pray for them and with them. It is my hope to establish a retreat center where pregnant women can come from anywhere and stay until it is time for them to go to the hospital, and where women who have had abortions can come and have the pieces of their broken lives put back together. The Sisters of Life will be there, praying for them, praying with them, helping them in every conceivable way. For what reason? Out of denunciation? Out of criticism? No. Out of love, out of the love that casts out fear.

Last year, on this same day, I said that in my judgment—and it is only my judgment—had abortion been legalized in his day, the Reverend Dr. Martin Luther King, Jr., would have taken the same attitude toward it that he took toward the taking of any human life. Within the next few days I was severely criticized for putting words into Dr. King's mouth (which I did not do). But the part that seems shocking to me is that it should be considered an insult to suggest that the best known civil rights leader in American history—had he been familiar with the problems of abortion, euthanasia, and assisted suicide, as we are today—would have come down on the side of life! I think that that is a grand compliment. I certainly do not consider it an insult.

I did not have the privilege of knowing Dr. King. Even so, I know of his ministry and his words. And the words that I will now quote are from a text called *The Words of Martin Luther King, Jr.* Dr. King says, for example, "Racism is a philosophy based on a contempt for life." He says, and to me this is a marvelous quotation, "I am convinced that if we succumb to the temptation to use violence in our struggle for freedom, unborn generations will be the recipients of a long and desolate night of bitterness and our chief legacy to them will be a never-ending reign of chaos."[3]

Many women struggle to be free. That is a perfectly legitimate struggle. They fear being restricted. They fear being oppressed, and with good reason. But if we succumb to the temptation to use violence in our struggle for freedom, the violence of putting to death an infant that seems to be restricting or oppressing or burdening us, then all we are going to do is introduce chaos for our children and for the generations yet unborn.

I believe what Dr. King preached so powerfully and with no fear. The night before he was killed, he gave a remarkable address, in which, apparently, he had a premonition of his death. He openly said, "I'm not afraid of what's going to happen to me. I've been on top of the mountain and I've looked across into paradise." I do not think there is any question but that the day will come that Dr. King's dream will come true—that every human person will be treated precisely as that, as a human person—nothing more, nothing else, not as black, not as white, not as a brown, not as a yellow, not as a Jew, not as a Protestant, not as a Catholic, but as a child of God. I believe that that will happen because when people like the Reverend Dr. Martin Luther King, Jr., lay down their lives for a just and righteous cause, God does not abandon that cause.

I believe with equal fervor that the cause of human life itself will prevail. I believe that, in the end, the Roman Catholic Church's teaching will be vindicated. I believe that all of those who have joined in the struggle to preserve, to protect, and to enhance the dignity and the sacredness of every human life will prevail. They will overcome. Even as the Reverend Dr. Martin Luther King, Jr., will one day overcome, despite the assassin's bullet.

I am very deeply grateful to all of you who are committed to the cause of human life. This, to me, is to be committed to the cause of citizenship, to the cause of the highest ideals of our land, to the cause of human dignity. But most important, this is to be committed to the cause of the Gospel of Jesus Christ, to the casting out of fear from the human heart. Thank you for what you do. God bless you.

John Cardinal O'Connor is the Roman Catholic Archbishop of New York. This sermon, presented here in unedited form, was preached on January 17, 1993, at St. Patrick's Cathedral in New York City.

Chapter 9

Am I My Brother's Keeper?

Frank A. Pavone

SCRIPTURE LESSON
Old Testament: Genesis 4:1-16

Some call it "the issue that just will not go away." The national debate over abortion continues to rage, despite yet another effort by the United States Supreme Court to settle the controversy—its *Planned Parenthood v. Casey* decision. The battle rages on, and it shows no signs of subsiding.

As the battle rages, some simply do not want to hear any of it anymore. There was the woman who walked into a sanctuary, took a copy of the church bulletin, and said under her breath, "I'll take this to read in case they talk about abortion." Then there was the senator who, in response to a letter about abortion, said that he would not even consider the question of when human life begins. And we—clergy, laity, citizens—have many other ways of protecting ourselves from information that makes us uneasy.

Cain and Abel

So did Cain, who committed the first murder in the history of the world. "Let us go out to the field," Cain said to his younger brother,

Abel (Gen. 4:8). When they had reached the field, Cain killed Abel. The Lord then asked Cain where his brother was. This had to be the most discomforting question that Cain had faced in all his years. How could he possibly stand up to God and explain the murder of his own brother? It was a question he wished would go away. It pushed him toward a truth too hard to face.

In a desperate attempt to dodge the threat at hand, Cain claimed ignorance. "I do not know," he responded. Then Cain went on to challenge God for asking the question in the first place: "Am I my brother's keeper?" (4:9). With these words, Cain tried to absolve himself of responsibility for his brother. Abel's whereabouts, his safety, his very life, were not the responsibility of Cain, or so Cain suggested.

At once, however, God called Cain back to take responsibility for his own actions against his brother. "What have you done?" God demanded (4:10). Cain wanted the issue to go away, but it would not go away. The issue was as close to Cain as Cain himself. It was his own action that took his brother's life. Yes, he is his brother's keeper, simply because he is his brother. Cain must respect and, if necessary, defend his brother's life. But Cain had done the opposite. He had held his brother's life in contempt. He had had no regard for his brother's very life. And he had tried to conceal his action by taking his brother into the field, where nobody else would see them. Yet God confirms that the deed cannot be covered over. "The voice of your brother's blood," God tells Cain, "is crying to me from the ground" (4:10). The issue will simply not go away.

Getting Beyond Cain and Abel

We are our brothers' keepers. That is not an option. Rather, it flows from our very existence as sons and daughters of the one God, in the one human family. We have responsibilities toward one another, whether we like it or not. We have responsibilities especially for the weakest and most defenseless ones in our society, the unborn, who are daily and violently taken from their mothers' wombs by abortion. We cannot claim ignorance of their whereabouts, as Cain tried to do. We cannot absolve ourselves of responsibility to them, as Cain tried to do. We cannot make the issue go away, as Cain tried to do.

A modern version of Cain's question, "Am I my brother's keeper?" is the common claim that we should "mind our own business." Wouldn't that make life easy? We would not have to be concerned about the sick, the poor, the homeless, or those with AIDS. We would not have to trouble ourselves about war-torn parts of the world, economic injustice, or exploitation of peoples and nations. We could just mind our own business. We would not need to hear about abortion, because the issue of justice to the unborn, and of justice to everyone else (besides ourselves), would just go away. We would have only our own business to mind.

Abortion is called an "issue of privacy." We are told not to interfere. This is yet another attempt to absolve us of responsibility to our brothers and sisters. The abortion decision does not merely affect the freedom of the woman making it. It is a life-or-death decision for the child in her womb. Our brother or sister's very life is at stake in the abortion decision. How can this be a privacy issue?

The Responsible Love of Jesus Christ

Our Lord Jesus Christ is ultimately the one who answers Cain's argumentative question and our arguments about minding our own business and about observing privacy. Christ teaches us in clear terms that we do have responsibilities to one another and that we cannot make the issue of injustice to our neighbor go away. Christ declares to us, "Love one another as I have loved you" (John 15:12). How did he love us? Saint Paul tells us that "God shows his love for us in that while we were yet sinners Christ died for us" (Rom. 5:8). In other words, God in Jesus Christ took the initiative. He came to us and died for us before our asking him and without our deserving him. We were totally helpless. He acted out of pure love when he saw our need. He made our plight his business. He did not assert his rights to privacy over against us. He did not hesitate for one minute. He did not ask his Father, "Am I my brother's keeper?"

As Christ loved us and loves us, so we can and must love our unborn brothers and sisters, and their mothers. We do not love them because they ask for it or merit it. We love them because they are our brothers and sisters in need. The problem of abortion is not solved by wishing it away or by ignoring it. It is solved only by active love. We *are* our brothers' and sisters' keepers.

Frank A. Pavone, a Roman Catholic priest living in Port Chester, New York, is the national director of Priests for Life. This sermon was first preached in the course of Father Pavone's rather extensive travels—probably sometime in 1995.

Chapter 10
One Little Word

Terry Schlossberg

SCRIPTURE LESSON
New Testament: Mark 4:35-41

Faith Facing Calamities

My father, now deceased, was an unbeliever, as far as I know. He rejected Protestantism outright. However, in spite of his rather tough skepticism, he kept a soft—though usually obscure—place in his heart for his Catholic background. His aunt was a nun, and during his last years, he invited her to visit on several occasions. On her visits she must have been wooing him gently toward the faith. Unfortunately, on one of her trips to see him, her plane ride was violently turbulent, and she became paralyzed by fear. She was so frightened, in fact, that she was not sure she wanted to fly again. Her report of the experience had a devastating effect on my dad. He realized that the little nun had been tested by impending calamity and that her faith had failed her. His disappointment was unmistakable. If there really were a God, he said to me, and she really were a woman of faith, she would not have been overcome by fear.

John Calvin, in his commentary on our passage from Mark 4, spoke to this matter of faith in the face of calamity. It was not the disciples' pleas for help that provoked rebuke for their lack of faith, wrote Calvin. Their crying out to Jesus, in fact, was a sign of their faith. But Jesus rebukes them by asking "Why are you afraid?" (Mark 4:40).

The Greek word translated as "afraid" in the Revised Standard Version implies that the disciples were *afraid beyond limit*. They had gone beyond the sort of fear that stirs faith, to a fear that, in Calvin's words, knocked faith "clean out of their minds."[1] They were desperate men who had lost hope. Jesus' rebuke reminds us that the sovereignty of God and the surety of his promises are never in question; and that he takes the sin of unbelief among his disciples, then and now, very seriously.

In their moment of testing, Jesus' disciples became like the complaining Israelites for whom God had made an escape by parting the Red Sea. This God also provided manna, quail, and sweet water when the Israelites were threatened with starvation and thirst, and preserved their lives by going ahead of them into the wilderness with the visible presence of a cloud by day and a pillar of fire by night. But in spite of God's repeated display of faithfulness, the Israelites allowed each new set of difficulties to overwhelm their faith. Each time they feared anew that they had been led out into the wilderness and abandoned to its terrors.

This fear of impending doom takes us back to the creation account to discover who is really in charge here. The Genesis story tells us that God is the author of all that exists and that he is the sovereign ruler over his creation. "The heavens are thine, the earth also is thine; the world and all that is in it, thou hast founded them," writes the psalmist (Ps. 89:11). Furthermore, the Genesis account speaks of God creating a universe out of a chaotic void and declaring it to be good (Gen. 1). In doing that, it draws a contrast between the Christian faith and the pagan beliefs of other religions: it makes the distinction between meaningful order and chaos.

The biblical history continually reassures us that God is in control of a universe that without him indeed would be chaos, without purpose or meaning. When the disciples cry out, "Teacher, do you not care if we perish?" (Mark 4:38), it is because their experience has persuaded them that God is no longer in control, that chaos has taken over again, and that they are lost. Hence, Jesus' rebuke, "Why are you afraid? Have you no faith?" (Mark 4:40). These men were firsthand witnesses of Jesus' sovereignty over circumstances in his many miracles. They had seen him cleanse a leper, heal a paralytic, and feed a multitude. But when their own lives appeared threatened, their faith failed. The extent of their fear reveals that they saw themselves as victims, alone, and without help in an empty universe.

Many of us fear the same thing. Some of us are terrified. And all of us at least sometimes find ourselves wondering whether the universe actually is an empty void, ruled by the chaos of circumstances.

Enter Nihilism

This view of a universe without ultimate purpose or meaning has a name: it is called nihilism. A great conflict between Christian truth and nihilism lies at the heart of the abortion controversy. The controversy over abortion is a conflict between the claim of purpose and meaning in the universe and the claim of nothing but chaos in the universe. Therefore, it is a conflict between faith and faithlessness, hope and hopelessness, love and lovelessness. In our age the choice of abortion is the clearest manifestation of the belief that we are alone, after all, and on our own in a hostile and threatening universe. All the language of autonomy associated with abortion—the my-own-body language—is ample evidence of that.

The candid writings of feminist Germaine Greer offer a concise expression of the nihilism that has produced the unsettling acceptance of abortion in our society. "The world is far from just," writes Greer. "Too many women are forced to abort by poverty, by their menfolk, by their parents."[2] The problem is not women who do not want their babies, she notes, but an "unjust world" that does not want them. And Lutheran theologian Paul Hinlicky adds that the injustice is compounded by a world that isolates women and lays on them both the responsibility and the blame for "sparing that unloved new life the terrors of [the world's] own lovelessness."[3] That is nihilism in a nutshell.

At the Presbyterian Church's national dialogue on abortion perspectives a few years ago, a participant remarked in a small group that the reason she is pro-choice is because she does not want the responsibility of caring for someone else's child. That remark joins the church to the unbelieving world in its declaration that the calamities of life sometimes result in the creation of human beings who are themselves without purpose or meaning, and that those sad, unwanted creatures are better off dead. Their deaths, in fact, become the means of salvation for the women who cannot bear the responsibility for their lives.

The current abortion position of the Presbyterian Church (USA) says this: "Problem pregnancies are the result of, and influenced by, so many complicated and insolvable circumstances that we have neither the wisdom nor the authority to address or decide each situation."[4] That statement speaks volumes about a denomination that is completely earthbound, standing in awe of the wind and waves; a denomination that has lost her ability to see the unseen with the eyes of faith; a denomination that can no longer declare the affirmation of the New Testament: "he who is in you is greater than he who is in the world" (1 John 4:4). And so, absolving itself of responsibility by its own lack of wisdom and authority, our church leaves women alone in the universe. Each year in the United States for the past two decades there have been at least 1.5 million of these "complicated and insolvable circumstances" that overwhelm women and press them to destroy their own tiny, innocent children developing within them. Abortion is a phenomenon of modern American life, claiming the lives of nearly one out of three children. It is surely an occasion for Jesus' rebuke to us as his disciples, in the modern church: "Have you no faith?"

Signs of Sovereignty

The psalmist, hundreds of years before the event in Mark, expressed God's ability to control a threatening universe:

> Some went down to the sea in ships, doing business on the great waters; they saw the deeds of the LORD, his wondrous works in the deep. For he commanded, and raised the stormy wind, which lifted up the waves of the sea. They mounted up to the heaven, they went down to the depths; their courage melted away in the evil plight; they reeled and staggered like drunken men, and were at their wits' end. Then they cried to the LORD in their trouble, and he delivered them from their distress; he made the storm be still, and the waves of the sea were hushed. Then they were glad because they had quiet, and he brought them to their desired haven. (Ps. 107:23-30)

And now, here in Mark, the psalmist's words come to life, and the Lord displays his unfailing faithfulness. The God who neither slumbers nor sleeps (Ps. 121) is roused by the distress of those he loves. And with one little word he breaks into the circumstances and brings them under his control. He stills the storm and hushes the sea, and the ship proceeds to its desired haven. And the gladdened disciples, preserved in spite of their failure of faith, stand in awe to discover once again God's sovereignty and his good purposes for them. The miracle itself, and the record of it passed down to us, is a mercy of God that gives us a glimpse of the nature and character of the ruler of this universe. In this account we are able to see what is ordinarily the unseen hand of God at work in this world, in his world.

This account in Mark—of God's power over the terrifying situations of life—flies in the face of the denominational claim that complicated and insolvable circumstances make abortion a necessity of life, however unpleasant. Those who framed that statement, and those who approve it, have not understood the rebuke of Jesus in today's passage.

The overwhelming numbers of abortions in our society stand as a judgment on the church for its faithless imitation of the nihilistic culture, for its awe of the stormy circumstances of life rather than awe of the mightier God. The church's statement leads the people of God into unbelief and dims the light of the church's witness to the watching world.

In this age of unbelief (or of belief in anything and everything), which may be described as post-Christian, we in the church would be wise to renew and proclaim our awe of the mighty and good God. And we would do well to express that awe in practice as well as in proclamation; in the face of calamity as well as in the serenity of the sanctuary.

Instead of joining in the isolation and rejection of the unborn and their needy mothers, the church ought to proclaim again that the life, death, and resurrection of Jesus Christ are the sure signs of God's concern for every human life, which Scripture says is created in the very image of God. And the church ought to be the avenue by which each newly conceived human being is received into the human community. We are the community that ought to boldly reject the view that the universe is haphazard and meaningless. And in faith we, the church, should become again what we have been in the past, and what Scripture admonishes us to be: a people that welcomes children.

Welcoming Strangers, Demonstrating Solidarity

A Presbyterian elder in a small community in Pennsylvania wrote me about his family's decision to welcome a stranger into their home. An unmarried teenager needed a place to live during her pregnancy. The elder discovered that the whole church community joined his family in welcoming the young woman and helped care for her.

As the day of the girl's delivery approached, the women of the congregation organized a baby shower, which many church couples attended. The men awkwardly looked around and caught one another's eyes, said the elder, and noted that, to the best of their knowledge, it was the first baby shower any of them had attended.

When the young woman gave birth to a baby girl, and when she decided that adoption would be the best alternative for the child, the elder's wife was with her. As it happened, the pastor of this little church and his wife were unable to have children of their own and were looking for a child to adopt. Before long, the new baby was delivered into their arms, and the whole congregation stood together in commitment to her spiritual upbringing.

The elder wrote: "We all participated as Kristen was baptized right here. Together we stood up as another elder read from the sacrament of baptism: 'Our Lord Jesus Christ ordered us to teach those who are baptized. Do you, the people of the church, promise to tell Kristen the good news of the gospel, to help her know all that Christ commands and, by your fellowship, to strengthen her family ties with the household of God?' And we said in unison, 'We do.' Later in the service the elder declared, 'This child of God is now received into the holy catholic Church. See what love the Father has given us, that we should be called children of God; and we are!'"

The critical problem of abortion presents us, as the church, with the opportunity of fulfilling our baptismal vows to the most needy among us. It presents us with the opportunity to extend the Lord's Supper, with its offer of grace, to their mothers.

The sacraments of the Church say to all that we are not alone, that we are not on our own, that we are not our own. We are bought with a price, and we belong both to God and to the community of believers, the Church. The opening words of the Heidelberg Catechism are a powerful denial of an empty universe without purpose and meaning. They offer assurance that each of us is wanted and loved. In repeating its words we affirm that our "only comfort" is "that I belong—body and soul, in life and in death—not to myself but to my faithful Saviour, Jesus Christ . . . that he protects me so well that without the will of my Father in heaven not a hair can fall from my head; indeed, that everything must fit his purpose for my salvation." The Christian faith strongly declares that we belong to God and to his people.

A Roman Catholic priest, Father George Clements, adopted a black child in 1985 and started a One Child One Church movement in black churches. He did this to encourage at least one couple in each congregation to adopt a black child. "The African says there is no child who does not belong to me," he said. And that ought to be our vision for the church: there is no child who does not belong to us.

Martin Luther wrote these familiar words in 1529: "And though this world, with devils filled, should threaten to undo us, we will not fear, for God hath willed his truth to triumph through us. The Prince of Darkness grim, we tremble not for him; his rage we can endure, for lo, his doom is sure; one little word shall fell him" ("A Mighty Fortress Is Our God," stanza 3).

The world is not spinning out of control. There is help available in time of trouble. Let us in the church be a demonstration to the skeptical world that we understand calamity as a test of what we believe about the nature and character of God. And let us show that because we are recipients of God's great mercy and benefits, we gladly accept our duty of loving our brothers and sisters. Under God's sovereignty and by God's grace, calamity can be turned into blessing. Amen.

Terry Schlossberg is the executive director of Presbyterians Pro-Life, based in Burke, Virginia. She is the co-author, with Elizabeth Achtemeier, of Not My Own: Abortion and the Marks of the Church *(Grand Rapids: Eerdmans, 1995). She first preached this sermon at the Presbyterian Church of Old Greenwich, Connecticut. Mrs. Schlossberg's sermon first appeared in* Fearfully and Wonderfully Made: A Collection of Sermons on Life by Presbyterians *(Burke, Va.: Presbyterians Pro-Life, 1995).*

Chapter 11
Children Are Special to God

Benjamin E. Sheldon

SCRIPTURE LESSONS
Old Testament: Psalms 127:3-5; 139:13-16
New Testament: Matthew 18:1-6, 10-11

God loves little children. Jesus declared that being like a child means greatness in the Kingdom of God; humble, childlike faith is what pleases God. Receiving a child is like receiving him, he affirmed. And the worst kind of punishment is reserved for those who lead little ones, dear and precious to God, into sin.

There is no doubt that God watches over his children, as Psalm 91:11 so eloquently promises: "He will give his angels charge of you / to guard you in all your ways." (These are the words Satan threw in the face of our Lord when tempting him to jump down from the pinnacle of the Temple.) We do thank God for all his protecting angels who guard our footsteps.

Nevertheless, when Matthew 18:10 speaks of "their angels" in heaven, it is more likely referring to the spirits of children who have died. Here Jesus is saying something like this: "Be very careful that you do not despise these little ones, for their destiny is to enjoy the undiluted glory of the Father's presence in heaven."

What Jesus is saying is that these children are precious in the sight of God the Father. They are so precious that they will continue in his presence even after they die their earthly deaths.

This is just what Psalm 8:1-2 means: "Thou whose glory above the heavens is chanted / by the mouth of babes and infants." Jesus quoted these words to the scribes and Pharisees on Palm Sunday, when they rebuked him for tolerating the children's loud, noisy hosannas in the Temple courts (Matt. 21:16).

People often ask the question, What happens to children who die before birth or in infancy? Grounded in the gospel and in the love of God, my answer is this: At the point of death, they become part of the praising chorus that surrounds the throne of God in heaven. There may be some here today who have lost children before birth or in infancy; if so, let this word be a source of comfort and hope to you.

In light of the incredible number of unborn children now being eliminated by abortion clinics in the United States, this passage offers a special word of comfort, hope, and even a measure of irony; for the more the devil rages, the more praise and glory God receives. As one

> whose glory above the heavens is chanted
>   by the mouth of babes and infants
> *thou hast founded a bulwark because of thy foes,*
>   *to still the enemy and the avenger.* (Ps. 8:1*b*-2, emphasis added)

Children: A Divine Blessing

I want to affirm, in the first place, that children are the special joy of God's heart. Today's Old Testament lesson, Psalm 127, puts it so clearly and declares it so emphatically: that children are a gift from God, a heritage of joy and blessing, a reward from him. There is a special blessing in children. It is one of the enigmas of our modern age that so many people fail to acknowledge that children are truly a divine blessing.

Mary Pride, in her book *The Way Home,* has a chapter entitled "God's Least-Wanted Blessing." In that chapter she describes the attitude among many husbands and wives who reject the idea of having children, and the way that many women, she claims, view their God-given role of motherhood as nothing but a burden. "With the advent of family planning in the 50's, motherhood began to be questioned," writes Pride. "In the 60's, the push was on for abortion 'rights.' In the 70's, abortion was legalized and motherhood became just another option on the menu of life. Today, motherhood has become a hobby. Couples don't want babies—certainly not more than one, or maybe two, and those [only] after they have paid for the new car and made some progress on the mortgage. When one or two have dutifully arrived, that is that." [1]

A few sentences later, Pride adds, "This spirit has crept into our churches as well. I remember how much it shocked me the first time we heard a Christian mother (of one!) complain about how much work her baby was and swear that she'd never have another one. That kind of remark is commonplace. Women, even Christian women, seem to feel no shame about rejecting the whole idea of motherhood, and their own children . . . along with it." [2]

It is quite amazing that secular writers notice and comment on this anti-child prejudice in our day. Germaine Greer, a noted feminist writer, devotes the entire first chapter of her book *Sex and Destiny: The Politics of Human Fertility* to lamenting and satirizing our modern lack of affection for children. She writes: "Historically, human societies have been pro-child; modern society is unique in that it is profoundly hostile to children. We in the West do not refrain from childbirth because we are concerned about the population explosion or because we feel we cannot afford children, but because we do not like children." [3]

In the modern age, the realization that children are a special blessing from God and that they are to be joyfully welcomed and desired has been lost amidst a secular mind-set and a materialistic culture that are essentially anti-child. We have forgotten that Jesus said, "Let the children come to me, and do not hinder them; for to such belongs the kingdom of heaven" (Matt. 19:14). To welcome a little child is to welcome Jesus himself. In the light of this verse, we must see what a high value our Lord places on children. Let us receive more, not fewer, of them. God wants to bless us with these special gifts, if only we would welcome them.

Unborn Children: A Divine Handiwork

Everything that we are saying about children being special to God applies to unborn children as much as to those who have been born. Some prefer to speak of pre-born, rather than unborn, children. In either case, that puts the emphasis on the fact that every child—after birth and before birth—is created, cared for, and loved by God.

The Bible is very clear that even before birth, everyone—everyone!—is a separate individual with a unique personality known to God. In Psalm 139, which is a part of today's Old Testament lesson, David speaks of how God was at work in him in a very personal way:

> For thou didst form my inward parts,
> thou didst knit me together in my mother's womb.
> I praise thee, for thou art fearful and wonderful.
> Wonderful are thy works! (Ps. 139:13-14)

David saw God at work in and through himself, even before birth.

Likewise, looking back, Jeremiah saw God's hand in his life long before his birth. The prophet claims,

> The word of the LORD came to me saying,
> "Before I formed you in the womb I knew you,
> and before you were born I consecrated you;
> I appointed you a prophet to the nations." (Jer. 1:4-5)

Isaiah tells us that even though a mother may reject her unborn child, even to the point of destroying her or him, God promises that he will continue to care for the rejected one. "Even these may forget, / yet I will not forget you" (Isa. 49:15).

It is clear from Scripture that God does have a divine intention in the creation of everyone, and children are no exception. He does know and love us before our birth; and every single human being—created in his image—is very precious to him.

In St. Louis in 1988, I heard Mother Teresa say this emphatically: "Every unborn child is precious to God." *Every* one! No exceptions!

Abortion: Rejection of a Divine Gift

Mother Teresa's statement that "every unborn child is precious to God" indicates that abortion should be resisted. Why? Because the willful destruction of an unborn child does violence not only to God's handiwork but also to the divine intention of the Creator, to the divine intention of the Redeemer, and to the divine intention of the Sustainer.

When we abuse God's creation, we offend God the Father. When we abuse the Father's creation, we deny the value of Jesus Christ's and the Holy Spirit's glorious work for all human beings, including those not yet born. Abortion is the most extreme form of child abuse.

The abuse of children is an abomination to God. God, who loves children, who gives them as blessings and rewards to us, who wants us to receive them in his name, will not allow people forever to reject or to abuse children.

Consider 2 Kings 17. Here it is recorded that the final downfall of the Israelites came because they had sinned against God. On the list of their sins, according to verse 17, was that "they burned their sons and their daughters as offerings." This had been strictly forbidden by Leviticus 20:

> Any man of the people of Israel, or of the strangers that sojourn in Israel, who gives any of his children to Molech shall be put to death. . . . because he has given one of his children to Molech, defiling my sanctuary and profaning my holy name. And if the people of the land do at all hide their eyes from that man, when he gives one of his children to Molech, and do not put him to death, then I will set my face against that man and against his family, and will cut them off from among their people, him and all who follow him in playing the harlot after Molech. (vv. 2-5)

Jeremiah 32:35 notes that Judah did the same thing and that God responded, "I did not command them, nor did it enter into my mind, that they should do this abomination, to cause Judah to sin."

Jesus will judge our regard for him by the way we have treated the vulnerable, the helpless, the weak, the ones whom he calls "the least of these" (Matt. 25:40). It is children, unborn and born, who are numbered among the vulnerable, the helpless, the weak, "the least of these." And God's loving-kindness, and the Church's, is always for these little ones.

Therefore, on this day, we must heed the warning that comes from the lips of Jesus himself: "See that you do not despise one of these little ones" (Matt. 18:10). For God loves children and empowers us to do the same. And in the end, God will judge us strictly by the way we have regarded children.

Thank God for children! And thank God who lovingly sacrifices for them! And thank God for his Son, for the gospel, and for the Church seeking the care of children.

Benjamin E. Sheldon delivered this sermon on January 22, 1989, at the Bethany Collegiate Presbyterian Church in Havertown, Pennsylvania, where he served as the senior pastor from 1979 until 1994. Sheldon is now the executive director of the National Pro-life Religious Council. Fearfully and Wonderfully Made: A Collection of Sermons on Life by Presbyterians *(Burke: Va.: Presbyterians Pro-Life, 1995) also includes this sermon by Rev. Sheldon.*

Chapter 12
The Woman at the Well

Paul T. Stallsworth

SCRIPTURE LESSON
New Testament: John 4:5-30

S isters and brothers in Christ, this is an important moment, a significant moment. Why? Because we have gathered together to worship God the Father, the Son, and the Holy Spirit. That is the most important activity that we as men and women, boys and girls can participate in in this life, in this world. Also, we have gathered together to consider how The United Methodist Church in particular, and the churches in general, might better respond to one of the most humanly destructive and devastating realities of our time: abortion in America.

Sixteen years ago, on January 22, 1973, the United States Supreme Court, located just across the street from this sanctuary, handed down its *Roe v. Wade* decision. This decision, for all intents and purposes, made it legal for any pregnant woman to obtain an abortion for any reason or for no reason. To this day, *Roe v. Wade* is still the law of the land, more or less, legally permitting over 1.5 million abortions in America each year. To date, the Supreme Court has yet to overturn or substantively revise this 1973 decision.

But this morning, the legality of abortion is not our primary concern. Nor is the politics of abortion our primary focus. Our primary concern, our mission, is to alert United Methodists and other Christians to the suffering that abortion is inflicting on women, men, and children in our churches and in our society today. Our primary goal, our mission, is to encourage congregations and Christians to be neighbors to those tempted or wounded by abortion.

Christ and Crisis

The Gospels describe how, during his public ministry, Jesus creates a crisis most everywhere he goes. When Jesus encounters the real people of his day—the clergy and the pagans, the elderly and the children, the soldiers and the revolutionaries—he brings a crisis on them. In the presence of Jesus, people experience a crisis because they have to decide. They have to decide whether to say No or Yes to Jesus and to what he offers them.

The fourth chapter of John's Gospel describes at some length how Jesus brings a crisis, or a moment of decision, to an anonymous Samaritan woman. Their encounter takes place during the lunch hour, during the heat of an ordinary Samaritan day. Tired and thirsty from his travels, Jesus stops at Father Jacob's well. Lacking the means to draw a drink of water from the well, he sees the local Samaritan woman doing her daily water-drawing chores.

Approaching her, Jesus asks her for a drink of water. But more important, he brings a crisis on this woman at the well. He spends very little time asking her for a drink of well water. Instead, he offers her "living water," and she must then decide whether to refuse or accept the living water that he offers her. If she refuses the living water, she stays with well water, and her life will not change. She will continue in her same old ways—changing husbands and lovers every so often, running and hiding from the women of the town, paying lip service to her religion. But if she accepts Jesus' offer of living water, she will be a changed woman, a new woman, a born-again woman, a "new creation." The Spirit of God will change her from the inside out, from head to toe. But she must decide. She must refuse or accept.

This woman faces her crisis head-on. She decides. She leaves her water jar beside the well. In other words, she leaves the well water behind. And she goes into town to tell people willing to listen about the One she has just met. She is a different woman, a new woman, thanks to the living water. Thanks to the Holy Spirit. Thanks to Jesus.

The Continuing Crisis

The Gospel of John emphasizes, again and again, that the ministry of Jesus goes on in this world even after Jesus has bodily departed from this world. That is, even after the risen Jesus Christ has ascended into heaven, his ministry marches on in this world. His words continue to be spoken and heard; his deeds continue to be accomplished and seen. "But how is that possible?" we ask. It is possible, says John's Gospel, because the resurrected Lord employs his Church to speak his word and to do his deeds. So the ministry of Jesus continues into the late twentieth century through the ministry of the Church, or so suggests John.

If the full ministry of Jesus is going on right now—and that is John's claim—then the Church, like Jesus, should be encountering the woman at the well and offering her living water. Yes, the Church—and all the churches—should be meeting the woman at the well and offering her a drink of living water.

In our day, we certainly have our own woman at the well. Of course today she will not be found drawing water from a deep well outside of town. Rather, she will be found working in a New York publishing house or in a clothing store, or shopping the aisles at the neighborhood A & P, or browsing in the self-help section of the mall's bookstore, or doing the laundry in an apartment building's basement, or paying a visit to the local "women's clinic."

In fact, the clearest case today of the woman at the well is the woman seeking the lethal services of an abortion clinic. She is often running from a mistake, an error, a sin. She is running from a future with a child, or another child. Perhaps she is left by a man who has used her and discarded her. She wants to keep her deeds secret. Usually she does not want her own mother and father, brothers and sisters, priest or pastor, to know what she is doing. So she goes, quietly and fearfully, to a clinic. This woman is today's woman at the well.

If the Church carries on the ministry of Jesus, the Church will strive to meet this woman—at the clinic, or before she gets to the clinic, or after she visits the clinic. Indeed, the Church, in the power of Jesus'

Spirit, will bring a crisis on the woman. The crisis will not come from the Church yelling "Murderer!" at the woman, as Jesus did not yell "Adulterer!" at the Samaritan woman. The crisis will come when the Church offers the woman a drink of living water, which will certainly include the love and support to help her bring her little one into the world. Then the woman will have to decide to stay with the well water and the same old life, or to take the fire water of the Spirit and new life in Christ.

If the Church faithfully carries on the ministry of Jesus, the Church will meet this woman and offer her living water and new life.

No Living Water Here

So, what about our churches today? Are the churches meeting the woman at the well? In the midst of 1.5 million abortions each year in American society, thousands of which are surely performed on church-going women, are we encountering the woman at the well?

The answer is No—not often. Most American Christians, it seems, are silent at best, and apathetic at worst, about the abortions being performed on the girls and women in their midst. Most church leaders—bishops, district superintendents, agency executives, and high-steeple preachers—think of abortion as an "issue" that is too hot to handle. It is "too controversial" and "too divisive," they say. So they attempt to silence the discussion of abortion, often by ignoring it. They themselves are careful not to address abortion. They see abortion as a nonproblem for their church.

And then there are some American Christians, though not many, who engage the woman at the well. But often they do not offer her living water. Instead they offer her plain old well water by encouraging her to abort. They understand abortion as a solution to problems—financial, educational, and psychological problems. Unfortunately, abortion is never a solution to a problem; it is just another problem.

Generally speaking, American churches are ignoring today's abortion plague. We have few homes that care for an unwed mother. We have few programs that support a woman with a difficult pregnancy. We have few ministries that help a woman through post-abortion anguish or injury, or through the sexual harassments that sometimes accompany visits to abortion clinics. We have made no concerted effort to teach chastity to our youth, or to practice it ourselves. In short, our churches are not meeting the woman at the well with an offer of living water.

The Difficulty and the Necessity

So let us be clear about this ministry at the well. It is a difficult, often thankless ministry. It is difficult for several reasons. For starters, the United States Supreme Court has declared abortion legal and a matter of choice. Therefore, with Supreme Court legitimation, the woman considers abortion a private matter and nobody else's business. Also this ministry is made difficult by the common reasoning that confuses what is legal with what is moral. Because abortion is legal, many mistakenly reason, it is morally acceptable. This ministry at the well is difficult for a third reason: many American Christians do not find it easy to talk about sexual matters. Yes, this ministry at the well is tough. It requires that we talk about something that is hard for us to talk about; and to make matters worse, it often requires us to talk to a woman who does not want to talk.

Still, this ministry at the well must go on. This woman must be offered living water. The Great Tradition of the Church, from the earliest centuries, has always understood abortion as an evil. We American Christians must now join the Great Tradition and the ministry of Jesus—which offers living water to the woman at the well—no matter how difficult the task. And we should have no fear, for the risen Christ will help us offer the water that he provides.

Do you see? Do you hear?

We cannot continue in our nonministry to the woman at the well. By not meeting this woman, American Christians are sinning gravely in two ways. First, we sin by not carrying out the ministry with which our Lord has blessed us. We thereby resist and disobey him. And second, by not meeting the woman at the well, we deny her living water and new life. We deny her the joy of salvation.

Offer That Water

On the back wall of this chapel is a striking painting of Jesus bringing a crisis on that Samaritan woman during a noon hour so long ago. He is offering her living water that she must either refuse or accept.

The Church can continue Jesus' ministry at the well. Today, Jesus wants to give living water to the woman who goes there. He wants to give new life to her, even as she is considering an act that would take the life of her little one and inflict harm on herself. And he wants to reach the woman at the well through his Church, even through our churches, even through you and me.

Brothers and sisters, living water has blessed us mightily. Living water poured out from the side of our Lord, while he hung on the cross, in our direction. Living water bathed us and washed away our sins. Living water came to us and filled us at Pentecost. And now living water sustains us on our way to this Communion rail, where we will meet the living Jesus Christ in the bread and the cup. But with the gift comes the task: now we can offer and offer and offer again the living water that we have received to the woman at the well.

O Lord, use your Church again to meet the woman at the well!

O Lord, use your churches, use us, to meet that troubled woman at the well and to offer her living water! Then she can truly live. Then she can offer life to her little one.

Paul T. Stallsworth delivered this sermon at the Simpson Memorial Chapel in The United Methodist Building in Washington, D.C., on January 23, 1989. He is pastor of the Rose Hill United Methodist Church in Rose Hill, North Carolina; editor of Lifewatch, *the quarterly newsletter of the Taskforce of United Methodists on Abortion and Sexuality; and general editor of* The Church and Abortion: In Search of New Ground for Response *(Nashville: Abingdon Press, 1993). An earlier version of this sermon first appeared in* The Human Life Review *(vol. XV, no. 2 [Spring 1989], pp. 99-103).*

Chapter 13

Whatever You Did unto One of the Least, You Did unto Me

Mother Teresa of Calcutta

SCRIPTURE LESSONS
Old Testament: Isaiah 49:15
New Testament: Matthew 25:31-46

On the last day, Jesus will say to those on His right hand, "Come . . . for I was hungry and you gave me food, I was thirsty and you gave me drink, I was a stranger and you welcomed me" (Matt. 25:34-35). Then Jesus will turn to those on His left hand and say, "Depart from me . . . for I was hungry and you gave me no food, I was thirsty and you gave me no drink, I was a stranger and you did not welcome me" (Matt. 25:41-43). These will ask him, "Lord, when did we see thee hungry or thirsty or a stranger . . . and did not minister to thee?" (Matt. 25:44) And Jesus will answer them, "Truly, I say to you, as you did it not to one of the least of these, you did it not to me" (Matt. 25:45).

As we have gathered here to pray together, I think it will be beautiful if we begin with a prayer that expresses very well what Jesus wants us to do for the least. St. Francis of Assisi understood very well these words of Jesus, and his life is very well expressed by a prayer. And this prayer, which we say every day after Holy Communion, always surprises me very much, because it is very fitting for each one of us. And I always wonder whether eight hundred years ago when St. Francis lived, they had the same difficulties that we have today. I think that some of you already have this prayer of peace—so we will pray it together.

> Lord, make us instruments of thy peace.
> Where there is hatred, let us sow love;
> where there is injury, pardon;
> where there is discord, union;
> where there is doubt, faith;
> where there is despair, hope;
> where there is darkness, light;
> where there is sadness, joy;
> for thy mercy and for thy truth's sake. Amen.

Let us thank God for the opportunity He has given us today to have come here to pray together. We have come here especially to pray for peace, joy, and love. We are reminded that Jesus came to bring the good news to the poor. He had told us what is that good news when He said: "Peace I leave with you; my peace I give to you" (John 14:27). He came not to give the peace of the world, which is only that we don't bother each other. He came to give the peace of heart, which comes from loving—from doing good to others.

And God loved the world so much that He gave His Son—it was a giving. God gave His Son to the Virgin Mary, and what did she do with Him? As soon as Jesus came into Mary's life, immediately she went in haste to give that good news. And as she came into the house of her cousin, Elizabeth, Scripture tells us that the unborn child—the child in the womb of Elizabeth—leapt with joy. While still in the womb of Mary—Jesus brought peace to John the Baptist, who leapt for joy in the womb of Elizabeth.

And as if that were not enough, as if it were not enough that God the Son should become one of us and bring peace and joy while still in the womb of Mary, Jesus also died on the Cross to show that greater love. He died for you and for me, and for that leper and for that man dying of hunger and that naked person lying in the street, not only of Calcutta, but of Africa, and everywhere. Our Sisters serve these poor people in 105 countries throughout the world. Jesus insisted that we love one another as He loves each one of us. Jesus gave His life to love us and He tells us that we also have to give whatever it takes to do good to one another. And in the Gospel Jesus says very clearly: "Love one another; even as I have loved you" (John 13:34).

Jesus died on the Cross because that is what it took for Him to do good to us—to save us from our selfishness in sin. He gave up everything to do the Father's will—to show us that we too must be willing to give up everything to do God's will—to love one another as He loves each of us. If we are not willing to give whatever it takes to do good to one another, sin is still in us. That is why we too must give to each other until it hurts.

It is not enough for us to say, "I love God," but I also have to love my neighbor. St. John says that you are a liar if you say you love God and you don't love your neighbor. How can you love God whom you do not see, if you do not love your neighbor whom you see, whom you touch, with whom you live? (1 John 4). And so it is very important for us to realize that love, to be true, has to hurt. I must be willing to give whatever it takes not to harm other people and, in fact, to do good to them. This requires that I be willing to give until it hurts. Otherwise, there is no true love in me and I bring injustice, not peace, to those around me.

It hurt Jesus to love us. We have been created in His image for greater things, to love and to be loved. We must "put on Christ," as Scripture tells us. And so, we have been created to love as He loves us. Jesus makes Himself the hungry one, the naked one, the homeless one, the unwanted one, and He says, "You did it to me." On the last day He will say to those on His right, "Whatever you did to the least of these, you did to me"; and He will also say to those on His left, "Whatever you neglected to do for the least of these, you neglected to do it for me."

When He was dying on the Cross, Jesus said, "I thirst" (John 19:28). Jesus is thirsting for our love, and this is the thirst of everyone, poor and rich alike. We all thirst for the love of others, that they go out of their way to avoid harming us and to do good to us. This is the meaning of true love, to give until it hurts.

I can never forget the experience I had in visiting a home where they kept all these old parents of sons and daughters who had just put them into an institution and forgotten them—maybe. I saw that in that home these old people had everything—good food, a comfortable place, television, everything, but everyone was looking toward the door. And I did not see a single one with a smile on the face. I turned to Sister and I asked, "Why do these people who have every comfort here, why are they all looking toward the door? Why are they not smiling?"

I am so used to seeing the smiles on our people; even the dying ones smile. And Sister said, "This is the way it is nearly every day. They are expecting; they are hoping that a son or daughter will come to visit them. They are hurt because they are forgotten." And see, this neglect to love brings spiritual poverty. Maybe in our own family we have somebody who is feeling lonely, who is feeling sick, who is feeling worried. Are we there? Are we willing to give until it hurts in order to be with our families, or do we put our own interests first? These are the questions we must ask ourselves, especially as we begin this year of the family. We must remember that love begins at home, and we must also remember that "the future of humanity passes through the family."

I was surprised in the West to see so many young boys and girls given to drugs. And I tried to find out why. Why is it like that, when those in the West have so many more things than those in the East? And the answer was, "Because there is no one in the family to receive them." Our children depend on us for everything—their health, their nutrition, their security, their coming to know and love God. For all of this, they look to us with trust, hope, and expectation. But often father and mother are so busy, they have no time for their children, or perhaps they are not even married or have given up on their marriage. So the children go to the streets and get involved in drugs or other things. We are talking of love of the child, which is where love and peace must begin. These are the things that break peace.

But I feel that the greatest destroyer of peace today is abortion, because it is a war against the child, a direct killing of the innocent child, murder by the mother herself. And if we accept that a mother can kill even her own child, how can we tell other people not to kill one another? How do we persuade a woman not to have an abortion? As always, we must persuade her with love, and we remind ourselves that love means to be willing to give until it hurts. Jesus gave even His life to love us. So, the mother who is thinking of abortion should be helped to love, that is, to give until it hurts her plans, or her free time, to respect the life of her child. The father of that child, whoever he is, must also give until it hurts.

By abortion, the mother does not learn to love, but kills even her own child to solve her problems. And, by abortion, the father is told that he does not have to take any responsibility at all for the child he has brought into the world. That father is likely to put other women into the same trouble. So abortion just leads to more abortion. Any country that accepts abortion is not teaching its people to love, but to use any violence to get what they want. This is why the greatest destroyer of love and peace is abortion.

Many people are very, very concerned with the children of India, with the children of Africa, where quite a few die of hunger, and so on. Many people are also concerned about all the violence in this great country of the United States. These concerns are very good. But often these same people are not concerned with the millions who are being killed by the deliberate decision of their own mothers. And this is what is the greatest destroyer of peace today—abortion, which brings people to such blindness.

And for this I appeal in India and I appeal everywhere—"Let us bring the child back." The child is God's gift to the family. Each child is created in the special image and likeness of God for greater things—to love and to be loved. In this year of the family we must bring the child back to the center of our care and concern. This is the only way that our world can survive, because our children are the only hope for the future. As older people are called to God, only their children can take their places.

But what does God say to us? He says,

Can a woman forget her sucking child,
    that she should have no compassion on the son of her womb?
Even these may forget,
    yet I will not forget you.
Behold, I have graven you on the palms of my hands. (Isa. 49:15-16)

We are carved in the palm of His hand; that unborn child has been carved in the hand of God from conception and is called by God to love and to be loved, not only now in this life, but forever. God can never forget us.

I will tell you something beautiful. We are fighting abortion by adoption—by care of the mother and adoption for her baby. We have saved thousands of lives. We have sent word to the clinics, to the hospitals and police stations: "Please don't destroy the child; we will take the child." So we always have someone tell the mothers in trouble, "Come, we will take care of you; we will get a home for your child."

And we have a tremendous demand from couples who cannot have a child—but I never give a child to a couple which has done something not to have a child. Jesus said, "Whoever receives one such child in my name receives me" (Matt. 18:5). By adopting a child, a couple receives Jesus; but by aborting a child, a couple refuses to receive Jesus.

Please don't kill the child. I want the child. Please give me the child. I am willing to accept any child who would be aborted and to give that child to a married couple who will love the child and be loved by the child. From our children's home in Calcutta alone, we have saved over three thousand children from abortion. These children have brought such love and joy to their adopting parents and have grown up so full of love and joy.

I know that couples have to plan their family and for that there is natural family planning. The way to plan the family is natural family planning, not contraception. In destroying the power of giving life, through contraception, a husband or wife is doing something to self. This turns the attention to self and so it destroys the gift of love in him or her. In loving, the husband and wife must turn the attention to each other, as happens in natural family planning, and not to self, as happens in contraception. Once that living love is destroyed by contraception, abortion follows very easily.

I also know that there are great problems in the world—that many spouses do not love each other enough to practice natural family planning. We cannot solve all the problems in the world, but let us never bring in the worst problem of all, and that is to destroy love. And this is what happens when we tell people to practice contraception and abortion.

The poor are very great people. They can teach us so many beautiful things. Once one of them came to thank us for teaching her natural family planning and said, "You people who have practiced chastity, you are the best people to teach us natural family planning because it is nothing more than self-control out of love for each other." And what this poor person said is very true. These poor people maybe have nothing to eat, maybe they have not a home to live in, but they can still be great people when they are spiritually rich.

When I pick up a person from the street, hungry, I give him a plate of rice, a piece of bread. But a person who is shut out, who feels unwanted, unloved, terrified, the person who has been thrown out of society—that spiritual poverty is much harder to overcome. And abortion, which often follows from contraception, brings a people to be spiritually poor, and that is the worst poverty and the most difficult to overcome.

Those who are materially poor can be very wonderful people. One evening we went out and we picked up four people from the street. And one of them was in a most terrible condition. I told the Sisters: "You take care of the other three; I will take care of the one who looks worse." So I did for her all that my love can do. I put her in bed, and there was such a beautiful smile on her face. She took hold of my hand, as she said two words only—"thank you"—and she died.

I could not help but examine my conscience before her. And I asked, "What would I say if I were in her place?" And my answer was very simple. I would have tried to draw a little attention to myself. I would have said, "I am hungry, I am dying, I am cold, I am in pain," or something. But she gave me much more; she gave me her grateful love. And she died with a smile on her face.

Then there was the man we picked up from the drain, half eaten by worms and, after we had brought him to the home, he only said, "I have lived like an animal in the street, but I am going to die as an angel, loved and cared for." Then, after we had removed all the worms from his body, all he said, with a big smile, was, "Sister, I am going home to God"—and he died. It was so wonderful to see the greatness of that man who could speak like that without blaming anybody, without comparing anything. Like an angel. This is the greatness of people who are spiritually rich even when they are materially poor.

We are not social workers. We may be doing social work in the eyes of some people, but we must be contemplatives in the heart of the world. For we must bring that presence of God into your family, for the family that prays together, stays together. There is so much hatred, so much misery, and we with our prayer, with our sacrifice, are beginning at home. Love begins at home, and it is not how much we do, but how much love we put into what we do.

If we are contemplatives in the heart of the world with all its problems, these problems can never discourage us. We must always remember what God tells us in Scripture: "Even if a mother could forget the child in her womb"—something impossible, but even if she could forget—"I will never forget you" (Isa. 49:15 paraphrase).

And so here I am talking with you. I want you to find the poor here, right in your own home first. And begin love there. Bring that good news to your own people first. And find out about your next-door neighbors. Do you know who they are?

I had the most extraordinary experience of love of neighbor with a Hindu family. A gentleman came to our house and said, "Mother Teresa, there is a family which has not eaten for so long. Do something." So I took some rice and went there immediately. And I saw the children. Their eyes were shining with hunger. I don't know if you have ever seen hunger. But I have seen it very often. And the mother of the family took the rice I gave her and went out. When she came back, I asked her, "Where did you go? What did you do?" And she gave me a very simple answer: "They are hungry also." What struck me was that she knew—and who are they? A Muslim family—and she knew. I didn't bring any more rice that evening because I wanted them, Hindus and Muslims, to enjoy the joy of sharing.

But there were those children, radiating joy, sharing the joy and peace with their mother because she had the love to give until it hurts. And you see this is where love begins—at home in the family.

So, as the example of this family shows, God will never forget us and there is something you and I can always do. We can keep the joy of loving Jesus in our hearts, and share that joy with all we come in contact with. Let us make that one point—that no child will be unwanted, unloved, uncared for, or killed and thrown away. And give until it hurts—with a smile.

Because I talk so much of giving with a smile, once a professor from the United States asked me, "Are you married?" And I said, "Yes, and I find it sometimes very difficult to smile at my spouse, Jesus, because He can be very demanding—sometimes." This is really something true. And that is where love comes in—when it is demanding, and yet we can give it with joy.

One of the most demanding things for me is traveling everywhere—and with publicity. I have said to Jesus that if I don't go to heaven for anything else, I will be going to heaven for all the traveling with all the publicity, because it has purified me and sacrificed me and made me really ready to go to heaven.

If we remember that God loves us, and that we can love others as He loves us, then America can become a sign of peace for the world. From here, a sign of care for the weakest of the weak—unborn child—must go out to the world. If you become a burning light of justice and peace in the world, then really you will be true to what the founders of this country stood for. God bless you!

Mother Teresa *is the founder of the Missionaries of Charity, a Roman Catholic order. She ministers in Calcutta, India, and around the world. This meditation on Matthew 25 was presented on February 3, 1994, at a National Prayer Breakfast in Washington, D.C. It is presented here in unedited form, at the request of the Missionaries of Charity.*

Chapter 14

Morality
in an Immoral World

Charles E. Whited, Jr.

SCRIPTURE LESSON
New Testament: 1 Corinthians 6:12-20

Today is Sanctity of Human Life Sunday. It is a day when thousands of churches across our country are reflecting on the sanctity of human life. We begin our reflections by recalling that all human life—including the life of an unborn child, the life of a person who has a mental or physical disability, and the life of an elderly person—is a God-given gift. Each and every human life is created by God. Therefore, each and every human life is special in the eyes of God.

When we think about Sanctity of Human Life Sunday, we normally think about the horrors of abortion. We say "horrors" because the ending of a helpless, unborn child's life is a horrible event. And every year there are more than 1.5 million children killed before they are born. This is a senseless, horrible fact of our time and place.

I could go on and on talking about the tragic effects of abortion on our society. Abortion has indeed had an undeniably terrible impact on American society. But today, I do not want to talk just about abortion. I want to talk about why life is an "issue" in our society. I want to talk about the underlying reasons why abortion is a reality we need to deal with.

Beloved, this morning, we want to get at the heart of the matter. At the heart of the matter is immorality, and how immorality has affected our sense of morality. I believe that in today's Scripture lesson Paul gives us some clues.

Living Like Corinthians

It might be helpful for us to understand a little about the early church at Corinth. The Corinthian church was founded by the apostle Paul during his second missionary journey. From its first days, the Corinthian congregation was an immoral mess. Its members were into a little of everything; there were a number of abuses going on among the people of the church. (Of course, at the same time, in the same congregation, there were faithful Christians who were hanging on.) One of the Corinthian church's biggest problems was sexual immorality. The church wrote Paul, told him of the problems that they were having, and asked for his help.

Paul's First Letter to the Corinthians is a response to that church's stated concerns. In the first six chapters of his first Corinthian letter, Paul lays a foundation for all that follows. In the seventh chapter, he responds directly to some of the church's questions. What is especially powerful about 1 Corinthians is that it deals with specific issues affecting the Christians of that time and place. And yet when we receive these specific messages of this book of the Bible, we see their direct and immediate application to our contemporary life.

We want to deal with the life issue in the same way that Paul deals with it in our text. To do that, we should go to chapter 6, verse 9. There Paul asserts "that wrongdoers will not inherit the kingdom of God." That is, the unrighteous will not be saved, will not be delivered, from sin and death. Well, exactly who are these unrighteous people? Paul answers, "Do not be deceived! Fornicators, idolaters, adulterers, male prostitutes, sodomites, thieves, the greedy, drunkards, revilers, robbers—none of these will inherit the kingdom of God" (6:9-10 NRSV).

Notice that nearly half of the types of unrighteous people listed in verses 9 and 10 are sexually immoral or have immoral lifestyles. And what does Paul claim about these people? He claims that they will not be saved.

Living Like Corinthians, Today

What does this have to do with the life issue today? People today are looking for ways to justify their desires. They want to be able to do whatever they desire with no fear of any consequences. People who engage in homosexual acts want society to condone their sexual activities. Promiscuous and adulterous people want others, especially the churches, to say their sexual habits are okay. But therein lies the problem: these practices are not okay.

Even though Scripture tells us that homosexuality, fornication, adultery, and the like are wrong, some people have persuaded and assured some sectors of society that such practices are acceptable. Therefore, our government now encourages, and in some cases even demands, that the homosexual lifestyle or "safe sex" or abortion be presented in our public schools or to civil servants as viable moral options. In every state your children cannot get an aspirin in a government school without your approval; however, in many states they can get an abortion without your knowledge or consent.

We teach our children that animals are becoming extinct and that wildlife should be protected. However, we also teach them, or allow others to teach them, that unborn children are expendable. If you kill a bald eagle and are caught by authorities, you possibly will suffer a severe fine and a jail sentence. But if you kill an unborn child by abortion, you are simply exercising an alleged, protected, legal right. Something is terribly wrong here.

We now have a generation that has grown up knowing abortion not as a wrong but as a legal right. This generation has known nothing else. As human life is steadily being devalued, many are presently demanding that they should be able to kill, with legal sanction, the elderly, the disabled, and the ill. Dr. Kevorkian certainly says it is okay. But Scripture and the Great Tradition of the Church clearly declare otherwise.

The sad result of a sexually immoral, sexually disordered society is abortion and disease. The vast majority of abortions are done for reasons of convenience and selfishness with no thought of the unborn child.[1] What is more, over 45 percent of all abortions are obtained by women who have already had at least one previous abortion.[2] These statistics demonstrate that, for many, abortion is currently the crudest form of birth control. Also, sexually transmitted diseases are skyrocketing, especially among our youth. The sexual revolution of the sixties has bequeathed to this nation, and to our young people, a tragic legacy of death, disease, and emotional and spiritual degeneration.

Brothers and sisters in Christ, I do not mind telling you this is the most difficult sermon I have ever preached. It literally breaks my heart to think of the hurt and suffering in this society, especially among our young people. I hope as you hear this message, your heart will ache for them as well. But our society now accepts and condones sexual immorality. Thus, as it did with the Corinthians, immorality has affected morality. Many churches now say that immorality is okay and justifiable. Statistics gathered by the Alan Guttmacher Institute, the research arm of Planned Parenthood, state that around 85 percent of the women who have abortions affiliate themselves with a Christian denomination. What is more, 18 percent of those claim to be born-again or evangelical Christians.[3] Clearly, the immorality of the world has affected the moral integrity of Christians.

The Heart of the Problem

When the evidence is in and assembled, what can we believe is the heart of the problem? Paul tells the Church in the text. People just do not know what God has done for them in Jesus Christ. They do not understand the love that God has for them. So people search for love and acceptance in all the wrong places. They search for love and acceptance the only way they know how, and that is through immorality and, more particularly, through a misuse of the God-given gift of sexuality. The problem with that alleged solution is that it only drives them further from peaceful communion with God.

We should make no mistake about it: God will not have any part of immorality. He will never accept or condone sin. Therefore, if we are going to engage in an immoral lifestyle and try to justify ourselves, we cannot have true communion with God. For if we join ourselves to a harlot, we become one with the harlot. That is why Paul states that the immoral will not inherit the kingdom of God. On the other hand, if we join ourselves with the Lord, we become "one spirit with him" (1 Cor. 6:17). I would rather be joined in spirit with the Lord and know the love of God than be joined with the suffering and torment of an immoral lifestyle without the Lord—even if society claims the immoral lifestyle is okay.

God gives us the Holy Spirit. Indeed, our bodies are temples of the Holy Spirit (1 Cor. 6:19), of the living God. Paul emphasizes this wonderful truth in our text. Therefore, if God lives in us, our bodies are not for immorality but for the Lord, for our bodies are a dwelling place for God the Spirit.

Paul writes that every other sin that a man commits is outside the body, but the sexually immoral man sins against his own body. The apostle is contending that the sexually immoral person desecrates the very sanctuary of God. Therefore, sexual immorality affects the Christian's life like no other sin because it affects the dwelling place of God like no other sin.

Paul summarizes in 1 Corinthians 6:19-20: "Do you not know that your body is a temple of the Holy Spirit within you, which you have from God? You are not your own; you were bought with a price. So glorify God in your body."

Deliverance

Do we get that? We were bought with a great price. We were bought with the death of the very Son of God. Jesus suffered a horrible death, a death by crucifixion for us. It was a very painful and miserable way to die, but that is the great price God willingly paid that we might inherit the Kingdom of God. Jesus was raised from the dead to finish that payment once and for all. If it were not for the glorious good news of the death and resurrection of Jesus Christ, for the forgiveness of all sins, we would have no hope. But God paid the price, and so we do have hope. We do have life in Christ, because of his resurrection. So every Sunday, which is a little Easter, is actually Human Life Sunday.

Brothers and sisters, Paul tells us to flee immorality. He does not give us that advice lightly and then hope that somehow we can overcome temptations on our own. Instead, God gives us the ability and power to flee immorality. He has given his Spirit to dwell within us. When temptations come our way, we need to turn to God and ask him to give us the strength to flee.

People need to know that God is really out there and that he responds to the cries of his people. Yet one reason there is so much immorality and so many abortions is that we do not live with God as the center of our lives. We do not depend on our Father daily. We do not let our children see us in prayer. We do not let our children see us weeping before God. Instead, we teach them that God is way out there and that we are way down here. Perhaps at best, by attending church on Sunday, we simply acknowledge that he exists.

Beloved, God is not just way up there. He is right here. We are created by him to depend upon him and to obey him. Do not be afraid or embarrassed to let people see your need for him. Let them know that God does exist and that he will give us deliverance and victory over all temptations, including those involving sexual immorality.

I want to conclude this message by noting that among us today there may be people who have fallen into sexual sin, even people who have participated directly or indirectly in abortion. Some of you may struggle with temptations toward infidelity or pornography or homosexuality. No matter what the world accepts, condones, or promotes, God calls sexual immorality sin. But God also is ready, willing, and able to "forgive our sins and cleanse us from all unrighteousness" if we will but confess our sins to him (1 John 1:9). His grace is new every morning to enable us to resist the sins that so easily entangle us, so that we might emerge into the light of the deliverance that Jesus Christ has won for us.

God paid the greatest price to win for us this real deliverance from real sin. Let us daily turn away from sin by genuine repentance and receive God's full and free forgiveness in Jesus Christ. Then his mercy will lift the burden of guilt and grief from our shoulders so that we may truly glorify God in our bodies, and our hearts will be filled with thanksgiving and praise for the wonderful things he has done.

In Jesus' name. Amen.

Charles E. Whited, Jr. preached this sermon to the congregation he serves, Hosanna Lutheran Church, in Columbia Station, Ohio, on January 22, 1995.

Notes

1. SPEAKING THE UNSPEAKABLE

1. Pamela Maraldo, quoted in the *Richmond Times-Dispatch*, December 13, 1992.

3. REJOICING IN THE TRUTH

1. Bernard N. Nathanson and Richard N. Ostling, *Aborting America* (Lewiston, N.Y.: Life Cycle Books, 1979), p. 193.
2. Francis A. Schaeffer and C. Everett Koop, *Whatever Happened to the Human Race* (Wheaton, Ill.: Crossway Books, 1983), p. 113.

4. THE SOURCE OF HUMAN DIGNITY

1. From *Ralph Waldo Emerson: Selected Essays, Lectures, and Poems*, ed. William H. Gilman (New York: New American Library, 1965), p. 454.

5. FATHERS, FAITHFULNESS, AND FUTURE GENERATIONS

1. National Center for Health Statistics as reported in *The Index of Leading Cultural Indicators*, vol. 1 (The Heritage Foundation, 1993), p. 10.
2. Ibid.
3. Ibid.

4. Barbara Dafoe Whitehead, "Dan Quayle Was Right," in *Atlantic* magazine, April 1993.
5. Former Vice President Dan Quayle as quoted in *World* magazine, September 24, 1994, p. 22.
6. Dr. Norman J. Lund, "Father of the Fatherless: The National Crisis of Fatherlessness," in *Evangel,* August/September 1993.
7. Gary Thomas, "Abortion: A Men's Issue," in *AAL About Issues,* May–June 1993.
8. William A. Mahlone, "The Forgotten Family Member," in *World* magazine, January 29, 1994, p. 26.

8. COMMEMORATION OF THE TWENTIETH ANNNIVERSARY OF *ROE V. WADE*

1. Jim Bishop, *The Day Lincoln Was Shot* (New York: Bantam Books, 1955), p. 292.
2. James Farmer, *Lay Bare the Heart* (New York: Arbor House, 1985).
3. *The Words of Martin Luther King, Jr.* (New York: Newmarket Press, 1983).

10. ONE LITTLE WORD

1. *Calvin's New Testament Commentaries, A Harmony of the Gospels, Matthew, Mark, and Luke,* Vol. 1, ed. David W. and Thomas F. Torrance, trans. A. W. Morrison (Grand Rapids: Wm. B. Eerdmans, 1972), pp. 280-81.
2. Germaine Greer, *Sex and Destiny: The Politics of Human Fertility* (New York: Harper Colophon Books, 1985), pp. 219, 229.
3. Paul Hinlicky, "War of the Worlds: Re-Visioning the Abortion Dilemma," *Pro Ecclesia* (Spring 1993), p. 201.
4. "Problem Pregnancies and Abortion," adopted by the 20th General Assembly of the Presbyterian Church (U.S.A.) (1992), p. 10.

11. CHILDREN ARE SPECIAL TO GOD

1. Mary Pride, *The Way Home* (Westchester, Ill.: Crossway Books, 1985), p. 36.
2. Ibid.
3. Germaine Greer, *Sex and Destiny: The Politics of Human Fertility* (New York: Harper & Row, 1984), p. 26.

14. MORALITY IN AN IMMORAL WORLD

1. Indeed, according to D. C. Reardon, "over 99 percent of abortions are provided simply at the request of desperate women who hope that by eliminating their pregnancies they can eliminate their problems." See his *Life Stories* (Wheaton, Ill.: Crossway Books, 1992), p. 111.
2. Ibid., p. 165.
3. See *Family Planning Perspectives,* vol. 28, no. 4 (July/August 1996).